Jokes You'll Love to Tell

A Prescription for Laughter

Dr. David Goldberg

This book is dedicated to
Lauri, the love of my life who
wisely rejected the jokes
that should not be told.

Table of Contents

Preface

While compiling material for this book, the working title was *Cement-Time Jokes*. Outside of my work environment, that title has no meaning to anyone else.

So what are cement-time jokes?

I could simply say that they are jokes used to kill time, but that would not do credit to the strange circumstances of their origin.

As a family physician, I have spent most of my career dispensing medical advice and encouragement to my patients. About a decade ago, I diversified my practice by working once a week as a surgical assistant in my local hospital.

That may sound impressive, but it mostly involves holding retractors and cutting sutures.

For this part-time gig, I have worked almost exclusively with Derek, an orthopedic surgeon who, on my first day, informed me that one of my responsibilities was to entertain the operating room during cement-time.

I had no idea what he was talking about and began to worry that I was not qualified for the job.

Derek went on to explain that when replacing a joint, some components need to be secured using medical cement. During the minutes it takes the cement to harden, the operation is stalled. He said, "That will be your time to entertain the room."

"Your options," Derek informed me, "are storytelling, stand-up comedy, or crafts."

Initially I chose crafts. I used leftover cement to create small misshapen creatures while the OR staff called out encouragement and criticism in equal measure. It was fun and challenging, but soon I began losing my audience's attention. It was time to move on to a different form of entertainment.

I began researching jokes and rehearsing them for my wife, Lauri. If she laughed, the joke would be told during the next cement-time. But a good response was not an automatic endorsement of the joke. Having raised three high-spirted children, she dreaded the phone call from the hospital's Chief of Staff, asking her to come pick up her husband. Some very funny joke rehearsals were followed by "You can't tell that one!".

Over the years, many colleagues have contributed jokes during cement-time, and a few of my family practice patients have also provided some excellent material for this book. Having spent countless hours searching for good material, I have gained tremendous respect for people who can write good jokes and hope to do them proud in the retelling.

This is the second edition of "*Jokes You'll Love to Tell*". The first edition found its way onto the shelves of the gift shop in the hospital where I work. Within days, I received a surprising message from a young nurse: "I just walked into a room to provide care to a patient who despite his pain, was lying in bed laughing as his wife read him jokes from your book." It was in that moment I realized the potential of this humorous collection.

And who was the nurse who sent that meaningful message? None other than my daughter, Aidan.

Preface

The first edition of this book generated a surprising amount of media attention. During those interviews, I was consistently asked how humor combines with medicine. In response, I've added to this second edition a chapter titled "A Prescription for Laughter," where I relate my own experiences demonstrating how these two disciplines complement each other.

But this is a joke book and it's time to start laughing.

It only hurts when I'm not laughing!

A man walks into a bar...

A pirate walks into a bar with an eyepatch, pegleg and a hook in place of one hand. The bartender is intrigued by these obvious signs of serious bodily harm and asks the pirate, "How did you get that pegleg?"

The pirate replies, "It were many years ago. There was a terrible storm at sea. A great wave swept a shark onto the deck and when I went to kick its sorry ass overboard it bit my leg off!"

"Wow, that's horrible!" replies the bartender. "What about that hand?"

The pirate replies, "It were a few years later. We were outrunning a British war galleon and as our quickly retreating ship was pulling away, I raised my hand to give a farewell middle fingered salute, when a cannon ball blew my hand off."

"How unfortunate!" replies the bartender. "How about the eye?"

The pirate replies, "It were not long after that. I was pacing up on the poop deck when a seagull came outta' nowhere and pooped in my eye."

"And that blinded you?" asked the bartender. "No, 'twas my first day with the hook."

A very shy guy walks into a bar and sees a beautiful woman sitting at the bar. After an hour of gathering up his courage he finally goes over to her and asks, tentatively, "Um, would you mind if I chatted with you for a while?"

To which she responds by yelling at the top of her lungs, "No, I will not sleep with you tonight!"

Everyone in the bar is now staring at them. Naturally, the guy is hopelessly and completely embarrassed. He slinks back to his table where he stares dejectedly into his beer.

After a few minutes, the woman walks over to him and apologizes. She smiles at him and says, "I'm sorry if I embarrassed you. You see, I'm a graduate student in psychology and I'm studying how people respond to embarrassing situations."

To which he responds in his loudest voice, "WHAT DO YOU MEAN $200?"

A lady walks into a bar and sees a man with his feet propped up on the table. He had the biggest boots she'd ever seen. The woman asked the man if it's true what they say about men with big feet being well endowed.

The man grinned and said, "It sure is little lady. Why don't you come to my apartment and let me prove it to you?"

The woman considered that she might never get an opportunity like this again and was curious to find out for herself, so she spent the night with him.

The next morning, she handed him a $100 bill.

Blushing, he said, "Well thank you I'm really flattered. Nobody has ever paid me for my services before!"

"Don't be flattered," she replied, "take the money and buy yourself some boots that fit."

A man walks into a bar and orders five whiskies. He lines them up in a row and proceeds to knock them back. He Drains the first shot, skips the second one and tosses back the third. He leaves the fourth untouched and empties the fifth with obvious satisfaction. He then gets up to leave.

"Don't you want the others?" calls out the bartender. You've only had three of your whiskies."

"I think not." Replied the man, "I've just come from my doctor's office and he said that based on my health condition, I should only have the odd drink."

A man walks into a bar and takes a seat in front of the bartender. He asks, "If I can show you something you have never seen before, can I drink here for free tonight?"

The bartender thinks about it and says, "Well I have seen a lot of stuff, if you can genuinely show me something I have not seen before, I will pick up your tab tonight."

The man reaches into his pocket and pulls out a miniature piano and sets it on the bar, then he reaches into his other pocket and pulls out a frog. He sits the frog on a tiny piano stool in front of the piano. The frog adjusts the stool, cracks his little fingers and starts to play!

The bartender is just blown away by this and agrees that the man can drink for free for the rest of the night. Meanwhile, there is a wealthy businessman watching this unfold from a corner of the room. The businessman sees an opportunity. He approaches and says, "Excuse me, but I saw your frog and I was wondering if he was for sale?"

The man replies, "Sorry the frog is not for sale", and continues sipping his drink.

The businessman offers $10,000 for the frog, which the man again politely declines, followed by offers of $20,000 and

$30,000. The businessman finally gives up and goes back to his seat.

The man finishes his drink and asks the bartender, "Hey, if I can show you something else even more amazing, would you let me drink here for free next week?" The bartender did not think this was possible, but eager to be proven wrong, readily agreed. What could be more amazing than a piano playing frog?

The man reaches into another pocket and brings out a mouse and puts him on top of the piano. A few seconds later the mouse starts to sing along with the frogs' playing! The bartender is absolutely floored by this and agrees to honor his deal.

The businessman also sees this and again approaches the man. He offers $100,000 for the frog and the mouse, which the man declines. The businessman in a last-ditch effort says "OK, what about $100,000 just for the mouse?"

The man takes a sip of his drink and says "Just for the mouse? Yeah OK." So the businessman cuts him a check right there, takes the mouse and leaves.

The bartender says to the man "Are you crazy!? A mouse like that has got to be worth 10 times that much! What were you thinking?"

The man calmly sips his drink and replies with a wry smile, "The joke's on him, the frog is a ventriloquist."

A group of college kids walk into a bar. They proceed to drink heavily and become quite boisterous. One of the young men approached the bartender and with slurred speech said, "I bet you $100 that I can pee from the top of a barstool into a shot glass on the bar and not spill a single drop".

The bartender, eager to embarrass the preppy young man and earn some money, readily took him up on his bet.

The bartender put a shot glass on the bar. The young man stood on the barstool and managed to pull down his pants. The young man then gently held his penis, took careful aim, and proceeded to spray urine all over the bar, not landing a single drop in the shot glass.

The bartender roared with laughter and collected the $100 from the drunk young man. While he was receiving the cash, he couldn't help but notice the huge smile on the young man's face. The bartender said, "You just lost 100 bucks, why are you so happy?"

To which the young man replied, "I bet my buddy $500 that I could piss all over your bar and you would be happy about it."

A man walks into a bar and asks the bartender, "What's the wi-fi password?"

The bartender responds, "You need to buy a drink first." So, the man orders a coke and asks, "How much is that?"

The bartender tells him that it costs five dollars which the customer feels is over-priced but doesn't complain as he really needs some internet access, and asks, "So, what's the wi-fi password?"

The bartender answers, "You need to buy a drink first. No spaces, all lowercase."

A man walks into a bar, and he's really annoyed. The bartender gives him a drink and asks him what the problem is. The annoyed man says, "All lawyers are assholes!"

A man sitting in the corner shouts, "I take offence to that!"

The annoyed man asks him, "Why? Are you a lawyer?"

The other replies, "No, I'm an asshole."

A beautiful woman approached the bar in a quiet rural pub. She gestured alluringly to the bartender who approached her immediately.

The woman seductively signaled that he should bring his face closer to hers. As he did, she gently caressed his full beard. "Are you the manager?" she asked, softly stroking his face with both hands.

"Actually, no," he replied.

"Can you get him for me? I need to speak to him," she said, running her hands beyond his beard and into his hair.

"I'm afraid I can't," breathed the bartender. "Is there anything I can do?"

"Yes. I need for you to give him a message," she continued, running her forefinger across the bartender's lip and slyly popping a couple of her fingers into his mouth and allowing him to suck them gently.

"What should I tell him?" the flustered bartender managed to stammer.

"Tell him", she whispered, "there's no toilet paper, hand soap, or paper towels in the ladies room."

A guy walked into a bar with a monkey. He sat himself at the bar and ordered a beer.

The monkey began climbing onto the bar, grabbed some olives off the counter and ate them.

Then he grabbed some sliced limes and ate them.

He then jumped onto the pool table and grabbed one of the balls.

To everyone's amazement, he stuck it in his mouth and somehow swallowed it whole.

The bartender looked at the guy and said, "Did you see what your monkey just did?"

"No, what?" asked the man.

"He just ate the cue ball off my pool table – whole!"

"Yeah, that doesn't surprise me," replied the guy, "he eats everything in sight, don't worry, I'll pay for the cue ball."

The guy finished his drink, paid his bill, paid for the stuff the monkey ate and left.

Two weeks later the guy came back and again, had his monkey with him.

He ordered a drink and the monkey started cruising around the bar.

The monkey found a peanut on the floor.

He picked it up, stuck it up his butt, pulled it out and then ate it.

Then the monkey found a maraschino cherry on the counter and again stuck it up his butt, pulled it out and ate it.

The bartender asked, "Did you see what your disgusting monkey just did?"

"No, what?" asked the man.

"Well, he stuck both a cherry and a peanut up his arse, then he pulled them out and ate them."

"Yeah, that doesn't surprise me," replied the guy.

"He still eats everything in sight, but ever since he had to shit out that cue ball, he measures everything first."

A man walks into a bar and takes a seat. "what'll you have?" asks the bartender.

"A scotch please," responds the man.

The bartender pours him a drink and says, That'll be ten dollars."

The man replies, "What are you talking about? I don't owe you anything for this drink."

And so an argument ensues which rapidly becomes quite heated. A lawyer sitting nearby says to the bartender, "He's right.

In the original offer, which constitutes a binding contract upon acceptance, there was no stipulation of remuneration."

The bartender is furious and tells the man to finish his drink and get out.

The next day the man returns. "What the hell are you doing back in here?" the bartender demands. "I can't believe you've got the nerve to show your face in here again!"

The man replies, "What are you talking about? I've never been in this place in my life."

"I'm very sorry," says the bartender, "but the resemblance is uncanny. You must have a double."

So the man says, "Thanks. Make it a scotch."

A man walks into a bar and says to the bartender, "I want you to give me 12-year-old scotch and don't try to fool me because I can tell the difference." The bartender is skeptical and instead pours the man a glass of five-year-old scotch.

The man takes a sip, scowls and says, "Bartender, this crap is five-year old scotch. I told you I want 12-year-old scotch!"

The bartender tries once more with eight-year-old scotch.

The man takes a sip, grimaces and says, "Bartender, I don't want eight-year-old scotch. Give me 12-year-old scotch or I'm taking my business elsewhere!"

Impressed, the bartender pours him a glass of his finest 12-year-old scotch. The man takes a sip and sighs, "Now that's more like it!" and continues to sip contentedly.

A drunk has been watching this with great interest. He stumbles over, sets a glass down in front of the man and says, "Hey, try this one."

The man takes a sip and immediately spits it out, "Yechhh! This stuff tastes like piss!"

The drunk replies, "Yeah, Now tell me, how old am I?"

Business and Politics

A Grade five student comes home from school and diligently begins doing his homework. After struggling with the assignment, he approaches his father for some assistance. He asks, "Dad, I have to do a special report for school. Can I ask you a question?"

"Sure son." his father answers, "what's the question?"

"What is Politics?" the boy asks.

His father carefully considers the question and provides an answer that would draw from his son's own experiences. He says, "Let's take our home for an example. I am the wage earner, so let's call me 'Capitalism'. Your mother is the administrator of money, so we'll call her 'Government'. We take care of all your needs, so let's call you 'The People'. We'll call the maid 'The Working Class' and your little brother, we can call 'The Future'. Do you understand son?"

To which the boy responds, "I'm not really sure, dad. I'll have to think about it."

That night, awakened by his brother's crying, the boy went to see what was wrong. Discovering that the baby had seriously soiled his diaper, the boy went to his parents' room and found his mother sound asleep. He went to the maid's room, where, peeking through the keyhole, he saw his father in bed with the maid. The boy's knocking went totally unheeded, so the boy returned to his room and went back to sleep. The next morning, he reported to his father. "Dad, I think I finally understand what politics is."

"That's great son!", said the boy's dad, "Can you explain it to me in your own words?"

"Well Dad," replied the boy, "while Capitalism is screwing the Working Class, Government is sound asleep, the People are being completely ignored and the Future is full of shit."

I recently asked my neighbors' little girl what she wanted to be when she grew up. She said she wanted to be President someday.

Both of her parents, Democrats, were standing there, so I asked her, "If you were President what would be the first thing you would do?"

She replied, "I'd give food and houses to all the homeless people." Her parents beamed.

'Wow! What a worthy goal." I told her. "But you don't have to wait until you're President to do that. You can come over to my house and mow the lawn, pull weeds, and sweep my deck, and I'll pay you $50. Then I'll take you over to the grocery store where the homeless guy hangs out, and you can give him the $50 to use toward food and a new house."

She thought that over for a few seconds, then she looked me straight in the eye and asked, "Why doesn't the homeless guy come over and do the work, and you can just pay him the $50?"

I said, "Welcome to the Republican Party."

A volunteer for the Democratic Party is canvassing for his candidate in a rural district. He stops to talk with a farmer who is standing on the edge of his field. He asks the farmer if he will support his candidate. The farmer responds, "I need some kind of a formal speech if you expect to earn my vote."

So, the volunteer looks for somewhere appropriate to stand while he tries to persuade the potential voter. The only raised area is a large pile of cattle manure. Without hesitating, he climbs to the top of the pile and delivers an eloquent speech extolling the virtues of his candidate.

The farmer starts laughing uncontrollably.

Insulted, the volunteer asks what is so funny.

The farmer responds, "This is the first time I've heard a Democratic speech on a Republican platform."

An old farmer was getting his hand stitched up after an accident at his cattle farm. He and the doctor strike up a conversation, which leads into politics.

The old farmer wasn't fond of politicians and went on to call them all a bunch of post-turtles.

Not being familiar with the term, the doctor asked what a 'post-turtle' was.

The old farmer explained as best he could, "When you're driving down a country road and you come across a fence post with a turtle on top, that's a post-turtle."

The doctor remained puzzled and asked for further clarification.

The farmer explained, "A post-turtle didn't get up there by himself, he doesn't belong up there, he doesn't know what to do while up there, he's elevated beyond his ability to function, and you just wonder what kind of dumb ass put him there in the first place."

A politician, his handler and two women are sitting on a train. The train went through a tunnel and the carriage lights failed to come on. The carriage became completely dark.

There was a loud kissing sound and then the sound of a hard slap! When the train came out of the tunnel, the passengers all looked at each other. The politician was sitting there stunned with a big red handprint on his cheek. The first woman looked at the second thinking, 'He must have tried to kiss her and got slapped'. The second woman looked to the first thinking, 'He must have tried kissing her and got slapped'. The politician is thinking, 'Damn it, my handler must have tried to kiss one of the women in the dark, and she thought it was me and I got slapped'. And the handler is thinking, 'If this train goes through another tunnel, I can make another loud kissing sound and slap that pompous, womanizing politician again!'

On a Thursday near the end of a school day, a teacher tells the class that whoever can name the President who said a famous quote could have Friday as a day off.

The teacher asks, "Ok class, who can tell me, who said, 'There is nothing to fear but fear itself?'"

Cindy excitedly shouts, "FDR!"

"Thats correct Hana," said the teacher, "you can have tomorrow off."

Hana responds, "No thanks. I'm Japanese and we value our education, so I'll be here tomorrow."

"Ok then, let's give someone else a chance. Can anyone tell me who said, 'Ask not what your country can do for you but what you can do for your country.'"

Daniel shouts out, "JFK!"

"That's right Daniel, enjoy your Friday off." beamed the proud teacher.

Pedro responded, "No thank you, I'm a Mexican and we have a hard work ethic. I'm committed to school, so I'll be here tomorrow."

"Well, I guess no one wants tomorrow off. Let's continue with the next lesson." announces the teacher.

As she turns around to write on the board an angry little Johnny in the back of the room loudly mumbles, "Fuckin foreigners!"

The teacher snaps around and in a demanding voice asks, "Who said that?"

Johnny jumps up and shouts, "Donald Trump! See you losers on Monday."

Donald Trump is suffering a public relations nightmare, so to try to prop up his image, he spends an afternoon at an elementary school talking to kids in their classrooms.

In one class, he teaches the young students about the word: 'tragedy'. Then, he asks them to use it in a sentence.

One brave girl raises her hand and offers, "If a school bus carrying 20 kids drove off of a cliff and killed everyone in it, then that would be a tragedy."

"No," Trump responds. "you're close, but that isn't a tragedy. That is what we would call a great loss."

A few seconds later, a boy raises his hand and says, "What about if my friend was at a farm, and a farmer drove over him with a tractor? That would be a tragedy."

"No." Trump repeats. "That is what we would call an accident, not a tragedy. Anyone else?"

The entire class is stumped for a while. Then, finally, another boy raises his hand and says, "I know what a tragedy would be! If Donald Trump was flying in his private jet and it got hit by a missile, destroying the plane, that would definitely be a tragedy."

"Exactly!" Trump says, pleased. "Now, can you tell the class why, exactly, that would be a tragedy?"

"Well," The boy replies, "it definitely wouldn't be a great loss, and it probably wouldn't be an accident either."

An associate of Donald Trump, maybe a golfing buddy, told him that he had a fantastic dream the other night and that Trump was in the dream.

Trump, with his ego stroked, asked his buddy to describe the dream.

"There was a really, really, big, huge parade in Washington celebrating Trump." said his buddy, "Hundreds of thousands, perhaps millions, lined the parade route, and cheered and cheered when Donald went past. It was the biggest celebration Washington had ever seen. Really Huge!"

Donald was very impressed and said, "That's really great! The best!"

"By the way, how did I look? Was my hair OK?"

His friend said that he couldn't tell. The casket was closed.

This is a test. This test only has one question, but it's a very important one. By giving an honest answer, you will discover where you stand morally.

The test features an unlikely, completely fictional situation in which you will have to make a decision. Only you will know the results, so remember that your answer needs to be honest.
THE SITUATION:

You are in Florida, Miami to be specific. There is chaos all around you caused by a hurricane with severe flooding. This is a flood of biblical proportions. You are a photojournalist working for a major newspaper, and you're caught in the middle of this epic disaster. The situation is nearly hopeless. You're trying to shoot a career-making photo.

There are houses and people swirling around you, some disappearing under the water.

Suddenly you see a man in the water. He is fighting for his life, trying not to be taken down with the debris. You move closer. Somehow the man looks familiar. You suddenly recognize the doomed man. It's Donald Trump!!!

You notice that the raging waters are about to take him under forever. You have two options. You can save the life of Donald Trump, or you can shoot a dramatic Pulitzer Prize winning photo, documenting the death of one of the most powerful Republicans in America.

Here's the question, and please give an honest answer. "Would you select high contrast color film, or would you go with the classic simplicity of black and white?"

Children and Animals

A man notices a small boy wearing a fireman's hat, sitting in a cart being pulled by his pet dog. When he gets closer, he notices that the cart is tied to the dog's testicles. The dog appears distressed and so the man approaches the unusual scene.

"That's a nice fire engine," says the man, "but wouldn't the dog pull faster if you tied the rope to his collar?"

"Yes", says the boy, "but then I wouldn't have a siren."

For his birthday, little Johnny asked for a 10-speed bicycle. His father said, "Son, we'd give you one, but the mortgage on this house is $250,000 and your mother just lost her job. There's no way we can afford it."

The next day the father saw little Johnny heading out the front door with a suitcase. So he asked, "Son, where are you going?"

Little Johnny told him, "I was walking past your room last night and heard you telling mom you were pulling out. Then I heard her tell you to wait because she was coming too. And I'll be damned if I'm staying here by myself with a $250,000 mortgage."

An elementary school teacher is giving a lesson about the effects of media on the community. For a homework assignment she asks the class to cut out a picture from the newspaper that causes a lot of excitement and commotion.

The next day, the class is presenting their newspaper clippings and discussing the effects that the pictures have on the reader. Susie shows a picture of a political demonstration, and the teacher agrees that people can get quite 'worked up' by their political beliefs. Next is Steven who shows off a picture of the New York Stock Exchange during an active trading session. The teacher explains that the pursuit of financial gain is a major motivating factor and congratulates Steven on his choice of picture.

Little Johnny is bouncing on his toes asking to display his newspaper clipping. The teacher reluctantly calls him to the front of the class where he presents a blank poster board with a tiny scrap of paper taped to the center. The teacher leans in closely and sees only a small dot.

The teacher asks, "What is that?"

Little Johnny replies, "It's a period."

The teacher says, "Why does it cause excitement and commotion?"

Little Johnny says, "I really don't know, but my sister said she missed one and my mom fainted, my dad had a heart attack, and the guy next door shot himself."

A dog and a cat are having a heated debate about which species is the favorite of humans. The dog says, "Humans like us more. They even named a tooth (canine) after us. Naming such an important body part after us shows that they like us more."

The cat smiles and says, "You know, you're really not going to win this argument."

A mother and her young daughter were visiting New York City. The mother was trying to hail a cab when her daughter noticed several wildly dressed women who were loitering on a nearby street corner.

The mother finally hailed her cab and they both climbed in, at which point the young girl asked "Mommy, what are all those ladies waiting for by that corner?"

The mother replies, "Those ladies are waiting for their husbands to come by and pick them up on the way home from work."

The cabby, upon hearing this exchange, turns to the mother and says "Ah, c'mon lady! Tell your daughter the truth for crying out loud! They're hookers!"

A brief period of silence follows, and the daughter then asks, "Mommy, do the hooker ladies have any children?"

The mother replies, "Of course, Dear. Where do you think cabbies come from?"

A turkey was chatting with a bull. "I would love to be able to get to the top of that tree," sighed the turkey, "but I haven't got the energy."

"Well, why don't you nibble on some of my manure?" replied the bull. "It is packed with nutrients."

The turkey pecked at a lump of dung and found that it actually gave him enough strength to reach the lowest branch of the tree.

The next day, after eating some more dung, he reached the second branch. This continued daily until on the fifth day, the turkey was proudly perched at the top of the tree.

He was promptly spotted by a farmer, who shot him out of the tree.

The moral of the story: bullshit might get you to the top, but it won't keep you there.

A teacher asks her class, "If there are five birds sitting on a fence and you shoot two of them down, how many will be left?"

Little Johnny blurts out, "None, they all fly away with the first gun shot."

The teacher replies, "The correct answer is three, but I like the way you think."

Then little Johnny says, "I have a question for YOU. There are three women sitting on a bench having ice cream. One is delicately licking the sides of the triple scoop of ice cream. The second is gobbling down the top and sucking the cone. The third is biting off the top of the ice cream. Which one is married?"

The teacher, blushing a great deal, replied, "Well I suppose the one that's gobbled down the top and sucking the cone."

To which little Johnny replied, "The correct answer is the one with the wedding ring, but I like the way you think."

There are usually a hundred hens on a farm and only one rooster. The rooster's only purpose is for mating and is useless apart from that.

One day, a farmer decided that the current rooster was getting old and bought a new younger rooster.

The old rooster, upon seeing the new younger rooster, worried that he was being replaced.

"What are you doing here? This is my turf!" he said to the younger rooster.

The younger rooster replied, "You are old and I'm here to help and eventually take your place. Why don't you just give up and go to the corner of the field and rest."

Visibly enraged now, wings flapping, the older rooster retorted that he'll sooner be turned into a stew, than to retire without a fight.

"I challenge you to a race, ten laps around the field! If I lose, I'll do as you say and stay away till the end of my life. However, if I win, you are to leave this field and never return."

The younger rooster smirked and said, "You are going to embarrass yourself in front of the ladies, you old cock. Fine, you are on. In fact, I'll give you a twenty-yard head start."

So the race got underway, and the young rooster chased the old rooster round the field. On the first lap, the younger rooster is catching up...

On the second lap... BANG! The farmer shot the young rooster dead.

"DARN IT! Why are all the new roosters I buy, including the two previous, only interested in chasing and mating with the old rooster?!"

Mrs. Applebee, a sixth grade teacher, is teaching fractions in her math class. She posed the following problem to her students:

"A wealthy man dies leaving ten million dollars in his will to be distributed in the following way. One-fifth is to go to his wife, one-fifth is to go to his son, one-sixth to his butler, and the rest to charity. Now, what does each get?"

After a very long silence in the classroom, little Johnny raised his hand.

The teacher called on little Johnny for his answer.

With complete sincerity in his voice, little Johnny answered, "A lawyer!"

A seven-year-old comes home from school and tells his four-year-old brother that cool kids are the ones who know how to swear. "You know what?" says the seven-year-old, "I think it's time we started swearing." He proceeds to teach his little brother the words he learned at school and suggested, "When we go downstairs for breakfast tomorrow, we should start using our new words".

"Okay!" replies the four-year-old.

The next morning, In the kitchen, when the mother asks the seven-year-old what he wants for breakfast, he answers, "I'll have Coco Puffs, bitch." Without a moment's hesitation he receives a swift backhand from his mother knocking him out of his chair.

As he lay there, half stunned, tears rolling down his face, his mother attempts to regain her composure. She turns to the younger brother and says, "And what would you like for breakfast?"

"Dunno," he replies, "But it sure isn't fucking Coco Puffs."

A teacher in a middle school is giving a lesson about community. The children are asked to talk about their parents' jobs. Susie's mother is a nurse and helps the community by keeping them healthy. Steven's father is a dentist and fixes people's teeth. The kids in the class have parents in all types of jobs, and eventually it's little Johnny's turn. When he is asked, he tells the class that his father is a pimp. The teacher hesitates and avoids asking him to enlighten the class on the job's description or community significance.

When the class ends, she asks little Johnny to remain behind. Believing that he had made an error, she asks, "What does your father do in his employment?"

Little Johnny responds, "He collects money while the client gets screwed."

The teacher throws back her head and laughs, "Oh, your father is a lawyer!"

The coach called one of his nine-year-old baseball players aside and asked. "Do you understand what cooperation is?"

"Yes, Coach," replied the boy.

"Do you understand that what matters is, we win or lose as a team?"

The boy nodded, yes.

The coach continued. "I'm sure you know when an out is called that you shouldn't argue, curse or attack the umpire or call him a peckerhead, jerkface or an asshole. Do you understand all that?"

Again, the boy nodded, yes.

"And when I take you out of the game so that another boy gets a chance to play, it's not good sportsmanship to call your coach a dumb ass or shithead, is it?"

"No coach."

"Good." said the coach. "Now go over and explain all that to your parents."

Sally is a six-year-old girl who is asked to be on her best behavior during a visit to the hospital. She accompanies her mother as they go to provide comfort for her grandfather. Sally remains calm throughout the long car ride, the walk through the hospital lobby and into the elevator. But as the elevator doors open on her grandfather's floor, she can no longer contain her excitement and runs down the hospital corridor. She bursts into her grandfather's hospital room and rushes straight to the old man's bed.

"Grandpa, Grandpa!" Sally yelled excitedly, "as soon as mommy comes into the room, make a noise like a frog!"

"Why would you want me to do that, dear girl?" said her grandfather.

"Because mommy said that as soon as you croak, we're all going to Disney World!"

The sixth grade science teacher, Mrs. Parks, asked her class, "Which human body part increases to ten times its size when stimulated?"

No one answered until Jenny stood up and said, "You should not be asking sixth graders a question like that! I'm going to tell my parents, they will go and tell the principal, and you will get in trouble!"

Mrs. Parks ignored her and asked the question again, "Which body part increases to 10 times its size when stimulated?" Jenny's mouth fell open. Then she said in a voice loud enough to carry to the front of the room, "I think our teacher is going to get fired!"

The teacher continued to ignore her and said to the class, "Anybody?"

Finally, Elliot stood up, looked around nervously, and said, "The body part that increases 10 times its size when stimulated is the pupil of the eye."

Mrs. Parks said, "Very good, Elliot," then turned to Jenny and continued. "As for you, young lady, I have three things to say to you. One, you have a dirty mind. Two, you didn't read your homework assignment. And three, one day you are going to be very, very disappointed."

Three bulls overheard that the rancher was bringing another bull onto the ranch.

First Bull: I've been here five years. I'm not giving this new bull any of my 100 cows.

Second Bull: I've been here three years and have earned my right to 50 cows. I'm keeping all my cows.

Third Bull: I've only been here a year, and so far, you guys have only let me have 10 cows. I may not be as big as you fellows, but I'm keeping all 10 of my cows

Just then an 18-wheeler pulls up in the pasture carrying the biggest bull they've ever seen. At 4,700 pounds, each step he takes strains the steel ramp.

FIRST BULL: I think I can spare a few cows for our new friend.

SECOND BULL: I actually have too many cows to take care of. I can spare a few. I'm certainly not looking for an argument.

They look over at the third bull and find him pawing the dirt, shaking his horns and snorting.

FIRST BULL: Son, don't be foolish, let him have some of your cows and live to tell about it.

THIRD BULL: Hell, he can have all my cows. I'm just making sure he knows I'm a bull.

A magician was working on a cruise ship. Since the audience was different each week, the magician did the same tricks over and over again. There was only one problem: The captain's parrot saw the shows each week and began to understand how the Magician did every trick.

Once he understood, he started shouting in the middle of the show, "Look, it's not the same hat!" or, "Look, he's hiding the flowers under the table!" or "Hey, why are all the cards the ace of spades?"

The magician was furious but couldn't do anything. It was, after all, the captain's parrot.

Then one stormy night on the Pacific, the ship capsized and sank with almost all on board going down with the ship.

The magician luckily found himself on a piece of wood floating in the middle of the sea, as fate would have it, with the parrot.

They stared at each other with hatred but did not utter a word. This went on for a day, and then two days, and then three days.

Finally on the fourth day, the parrot could not hold back any longer and said, "Okay, I give up. Where's the ship?"

A little bird was flying south for the winter. It was so cold the bird froze and fell to the ground into a large field. While he was lying there, a cow came by and dropped some dung on him. As the frozen bird lay there in the pile of cow manure, he began to realize how warm he was. The dung was actually thawing him out! He lay there all warm and happy, and soon began to sing for joy.

A cat passing nearby heard the bird singing and came to investigate. Following the sound, the cat discovered the bird under the pile of cow dung, and promptly dug him out and ate him.

Morals of the story:

Not everyone who shits on you is your enemy.

Not everyone who gets you out of shit is your friend.

And when you're in deep shit, it's best to keep your mouth shut!

A lady goes to her parish priest one day and tells him, "Father, I have a problem. I have two female parrots which I rescued from the brothel after that depraved establishment was finally closed down. They only know how to say one thing and it's most embarrassing."

"What do they say?" the priest inquired.

"They say 'Hi, we are prostitutes. Do you want to have some fun?'"

The priest said, "I can see why you were embarrassed." He thought a minute and then said, "You know I may have a solution to this problem. I have two male parrots whom I have taught to pray and read the Bible. Bring your two parrots over to my house and we will put them in the cage with Francis and Jacob. My parrots can teach your parrots to praise and worship. I'm sure your parrots will stop saying that phrase in no time."

"Thank you!" the lady responded, "This may very well be the solution."

The next day she brought her female parrots to the priest's house. As he ushered her in, she saw that his two male parrots were inside their cage, holding their rosary beads and praying. Impressed, she walked over and placed her parrots into the cage with them. After just a couple of seconds, the female parrots exclaimed out in unison. "Hi we are prostitutes. Do you want to have some fun?"

There was a stunned silence. Finally, one male parrot looked over at the other male parrot and said, "Put the beads away Francis, our prayers have been answered!"

A mated pair of sperm whales are on their annual migration to the cooler waters of the Arctic Ocean. On the way, the massive male spots the hull of a whaling ship in the distance.

As the pair get closer, the enormous whale identifies the vessel as the one that killed his father. Incensed, he tells his mate that they must sink the ship.

She asks how they can do this. After a few moments the male suggests that they both fill their lungs to capacity, dive very deep and when they are directly below the ship, release all their air at the same time. He reasons that this will cause enough turbulence to capsize the ship.

She agrees and they proceed with the plan.

The ship violently rocks and then flips over spilling the entire crew into the sea.

The whale is triumphant, until he sees that the sailors are swimming for shore, and he turns to his mate and says, "I cannot allow these sailors to live, they are responsible for my father's death. Let's go eat them before they can swim ashore."

At this the female whale balks and says, "I went along with you for the blow job, but I will not swallow the seamen!"

A weary traveler is making his way through the countryside when he decides that it is time to find a place to stop for the night. He walks up to the front door of a farmhouse and knocks on the door. He asks the farmer if he can sleep in his barn, as he is just looking to have a roof over his head for the night.

The farmer tells him that he may not sleep in his barn, but he would be happy to give him a warm bed in his house to spend the night.

The traveler is so appreciative of the offer that he asks if he could provide some free farm labor to offset his intrusion. The farmer would have nothing of it and insisted that the traveler was his guest.

He instructed the weary man to get washed up and to join him for dinner.

After dinner, the traveler again offered his services, and his offer was politely declined. He was reminded that he was a guest, and that he should get some sleep so that he could get an early start the following day.

In the morning he was served breakfast. So happy was he to be treated kindly, he told the farmer a secret. He told him that he had a special ability to talk to animals. "Would you allow me to talk to your animals as a token of my appreciation?"

The farmer assumed that the traveler was a little 'off' and so to avoid insulting him told him to go right ahead.

The traveler headed out to the barn and returned about 30 minutes later.

He told the farmer that he had been talking to the horses. He said that the horses were not very happy.

Recently the bits had been changed from an oval shape to a triangular shape and the new bits were hurting their mouths, preventing them from pulling as hard as they used to.

The farmer was flabbergasted. "Yes!" he exclaimed. "That is exactly right. I will change back to the old bits right away."

"Great," said the traveler, "now I will go talk to the cows." He is gone a short while and returns with similar concerns from the cows.

"The cows are complaining that the settings on the automated milkers have been changed from 20 cycles a minute to 22 cycles per minute and it is hurting their nipples, reducing their milk production."

Again, the farmer is amazed and insists that he will change the machines back to their previous settings.

"Before I go," said the traveler, "I will talk to the sheep."

"NO!" exclaimed the farmer. "Don't talk to the sheep, everybody knows they are compulsive liars!"

A teacher is explaining biology to her eight-year-old students. "Human beings are the only animals that stutter."

A little girl raises her hand and says, "I had a kitty cat who stuttered."

The teacher, knowing how precious some of these stories could become, asked the girl to describe the incident.

"Well," she began, "I was in the back yard with my kitty and the rottweiler who lives next door jumped over the fence into our yard!"

"That must've been scary!" said the teacher.

"It sure was," said the little girl. "My kitty went 'Ffff, Ffff, Ffff'... and before he could say "FUCK," the rottweiler ate him!"

Dating, Marriage and Infidelity

A man meets a gorgeous woman in a bar. They talk, they connect, they end up leaving the bar together. They get back to her place, and as she shows him around her apartment, he notices that her bedroom is completely packed with teddy bears.

Hundreds of small bears on a shelf along the floor, medium sized ones on the next shelf up, and huge bears on the top shelf.

The man is kind of surprised that this woman would have a collection of teddy bears, especially one so expansive, but he decides not to mention this to her.

After a night of passion, as they are lying together in the afterglow, the man rolls over and asks, smiling, "Well, how was it?"

The woman says, "You can have any prize from the bottom shelf."

Bob found out he was going to inherit a fortune after his sickly father died.

He decided that his life would be more complete if he had a wife with whom he could enjoy the luxurious life that the inheritance would support. So one evening he went to a singles bar where he spotted the most beautiful woman he had ever seen. Her natural beauty took his breath away.

He boldly crossed the room and addressed the gorgeous woman, "I may look like just an ordinary man," he said, "but in the near future, my father will die, and I will inherit twenty million dollars."

Impressed, the woman went home with him that evening.

Three days later, she became his stepmother.

A young New York woman was so depressed that she decided to end her life by drowning herself in the ocean, but just before she could throw herself from the docks, a handsome young man stopped her.

"You have so much to live for," said the man. "I'm a sailor, and we are off to Italy tomorrow. I can stow you away on my ship. I'll take care of you, bring you food every day, and keep you happy."

With nothing to lose, combined with the fact that she had always wanted to go to Italy, the woman accepted. That night the sailor brought her aboard and hid her in a small but comfortable compartment in the hold. From then on, every night he would bring her three sandwiches, a bottle of red wine, and make love to her until dawn.

Three weeks later she was discovered by the captain during a routine inspection.

"What are you doing here?" asked the captain.

"I have an arrangement with one of the sailors," she replied. "He brings me food, and I get a free trip to Italy."

"I see." the captain says.

Her conscience got the best of her, and she added, "Plus, he's screwing me."

"He certainly is!" replied the captain, "This is the Staten Island Ferry."

A girl asks her boyfriend to come over Friday night and have dinner with her parents. Since this is such a big event, the girl announces to her boyfriend that, after dinner, she would like to go out and make love for the first time.

Well, the young man was ecstatic. This would be his first time and from his sex education classes, he knew he would require some protection. He went to the pharmacy where he stared at the display of prophylactics in obvious confusion. The pharmacist, seeing the young man's discomfort, tells the boy everything there is to know about condoms.

At the register, the pharmacist asks the boy how many contraceptives he'd like to buy, a 3-pack, 10-pack, or family pack. The boy insists on the family pack because he thinks he will be rather busy, it being his first time and all.

That night, the boy shows up at the girl's parents house and meets his girlfriend at the door. "Oh, I'm so excited for you to meet my parents, come on in!" The boy goes inside and is taken to the dinner table where the girl's parents are seated. The boy quickly offers to say a prayer and bows his head. A minute passes, and the boy is still deep in prayer, with his head down.

10 minutes passed, and still no movement from the boy. Finally, after 20 minutes with his head down, the girlfriend leans over and whispers to the boyfriend, "I had no idea you were this religious!"

The boy whispers back, "I had no idea your father was a pharmacist."

A guy decides to buy his new girlfriend a pair of gloves for Christmas. They've only been dating for three weeks so it seemed like the ideal gift; romantic but not too personal. He asks his girlfriend's younger sister to accompany him to the store, believing that she could help him pick a pair that her sister would like.

They go to the mall and the sister points out a pair of white gloves which the sales assistant assures him are a good choice. The sister then picks out a pair of panties for herself and buys them separately. But during the wrapping, the clerk mixes up the parcels without anyone noticing. The sister gets the gloves, and the guy takes home the gift box containing the panties.

He then composes a helpful note to go with his gift and places the wrapped package under her tree.

To my dearest.

I chose these because I noticed you're not in the habit of wearing any when we go out. If it hadn't been for your sister, I would've got the long ones with the buttons, but she wears the short ones that are easier to get off.

These are a light shade but the lady I bought them from showed me a pair she'd been wearing for the past three weeks, and they were hardly soiled. I had her try yours on for me and they looked really great. I wish I was there to put them on for you the first time.

When you take them off remember to blow in them before putting them away as they'll naturally be a little damp from wearing.

P.S. The latest style is to wear them folded down with a little fur showing.

A nice girl brings home her fiancé to meet her parents.

After dinner, her mother tells her father to find out about the young man.

He invites the fiancé to his study for a chat.

"So, what are your plans?" the father asks the fiancé.

"I am a Biblical scholar." he replies.

"A Biblical scholar, admirable, but what will you do to provide a nice home for my daughter to live in, as she's accustomed to?"

"I will study," the young man replies, "and God will provide for us."

"And how will you buy her a beautiful engagement ring, such as she deserves?"

"I will concentrate on my studies; God will provide for us."

"And children? How will you support children?"

"Don't worry, sir, God will provide."

The conversation proceeds like this, and each time the father questions, the fiancé insists that God will provide.

Later, the mother asks, "So? How did it go?"

"He has no job and no plans, but he thinks I'm God!"

A young man moved out from home and into a new apartment. Enjoying his newfound independence, he went proudly down to the lobby to put his name on his mailbox. While there, a stunning young lady came out of the apartment next to the mailboxes, wearing only a robe.

The young man smiled at the beautiful woman, and they started up a conversation.

As they talked, her robe slipped open, and it was obvious that she wore nothing under the robe.

The poor kid broke into a sweat trying to maintain eye contact. After a few minutes, she placed her hand on his arm and said, "Let's go to my apartment, I hear someone coming."

He followed her into her apartment, she closed the door and leaned against it, allowing her robe to fall off completely. Now nude, she purred at him, "What would you say is my best feature?"

Flustered and embarrassed, he finally squeaked, "It's got to be your ears."

Astounded, and a little hurt she asked, "My ears? Look at these breasts, they are a full 38 inches and 100% natural. I work out every day and my ass is firm and solid. I have a 28 inch waist. Look at my skin, not a blemish anywhere."

"How can you think that the best part of my body is my ears?"

Clearing his throat, he stammered ... "Outside, when you said you heard someone coming ... that was me."

An insecure guy went to a doctor to discuss the possibility of getting a penile implant.

The doctor said "You have come to the right place. We have a new procedure that has worked very well for several of our patients. We implant part of an elephant's trunk into your penis. I expect you'll be completely satisfied when the operation is complete, and the surgical site is fully healed.

Although the man was a little hesitant, he agreed to having the operation.

After several weeks of healing up, he mustered up the courage to call his girlfriend. "Honey, I'd like to take you out tonight to a nice dinner."

They arrived at a quaint restaurant that evening. It was a very nice setting.

They ordered wine and an appetizer. After some wine and conversation, while looking at his girl longingly, he was thinking about what they might be doing a little later that evening.

Suddenly, his penis jumped out, went up on the table, grabbed a dinner roll, and went back under the table.

He was horrified and apologized profusely. "I'm so sorry, I had no idea that was going to happen. Can you forgive me?"

She said, "Oh no, that was wonderful! Can you do it again?"

He replied, "Well I could, but I don't think my butt can take another dinner roll."

A young man moves out of his family home and into an apartment with a roommate.

After a couple of months, he finally gets around to inviting his somewhat strict mother over to his apartment for dinner.

His mother had suspicions that there was more to the roommate arrangement than just a shared space. Throughout the meal, his mother couldn't help but notice how pretty his roommate was, and this increased her suspicions of a relationship between the two.

Reading his mother's thoughts, the young man volunteered, "I know what you must be thinking, but I assure you that we are just roommates."

About a week later. His roommate came to him, saying. "Ever since your mother came to dinner, I've been unable to find the silver plate. You don't suppose she took it, do you?"

He said, "Well, I doubt it, but I'll email her just to be sure." He sent the following email:

> Dear mother,
>
> I'm not saying that you took the silver plate from my house. I'm not saying that you did not take the silver plate, but the fact remains that it has been missing ever since you were here for dinner.
>
> Love, Your Son

Several days later, he received an email from his mother which read:

> Dear son,
>
> I'm not saying that you sleep with your roommate and I'm not saying that you do not sleep with her, but the fact remains that if she were sleeping in her own bed, she would have found the silver plate under her pillow.
>
> Love, Mom

A hotel guest frantically calls the front desk, the clerk answers, "May I help you, sir?"

The man says "Yes, I'm in room 858. You need to send someone to my room immediately. I'm having an argument with my wife, and she says she's going to jump out the window."

The desk clerk says, "I'm sorry sir, but that's a domestic problem, you'll need to call 911."

The man replies, "Listen you idiot. The window won't open, that's a maintenance issue."

A woman peers into her bedroom mirror and sighs, deeply.

Her concerned husband quickly asks, "What's the matter?"

She turns around to face him and says, "I'm not who I used to be. My forehead is wrinkly, my nose and ears are gigantic, my lips are deflated, and my crows' feet are getting deeper every day! My arms are flabby and my breasts are saggy!" The woman hangs her head, tears in her eyes. "Please, honey, I really need you to give me an honest compliment."

The husband looks her up and down, then replies, "You have excellent eyesight."

My father and mother were recently celebrating their 50th wedding anniversary. While cutting the cake, my mother was moved after seeing my father's eyes fill with tears. Mother took his arm and looked at him affectionately. "I never knew you were so sentimental," she whispered.

"No, no." he said, choking back his tears, "That's not it at all. Remember when your father found us in the barn and told me to either marry you or spend the next 50 years in jail?"

"Yes," my mother replied. "I remember it like yesterday." "Well," said my father, "today I would have been a free man!"

A man set out to do some yard work. He needed to clean up after a big storm littered his yard with leaves and branches. He clearly wasn't the only person taking on this task, as woodchippers could be heard loudly throughout the neighborhood.

When he went to the tool shed. His rake was missing.

He could see his wife upstairs through a window and yelled. "Where's the rake?"

She couldn't hear him and shouted back, "What?"

The man pointed to his eye, then pointed to his knee and made a raking motion.

His wife didn't understand the pantomime and shrugged her shoulders to indicate her confusion.

He repeated the gestures: EYE KNEE the RAKE.

His wife signaled back that she understood.

She first pointed to her eye. Next, she pointed to her left breast. Then she pointed to her bum and finally to her crotch.

He could not come close to deciphering that seemingly random pattern of gestures. Exasperated, he went back into the house and asked her to explain.

She replied: EYE-LEFT TIT-BEHIND- the BUSH.

A man walked into a therapist's office looking very depressed. "Doc, you've got to help me. I can't go on like this."

"What's the problem?" the therapist inquired.

"Well, I'm 35 years old, and I still have no luck with the ladies. No matter how hard I try, I just seem to scare them away."

"I can help you with this problem. You just need to work on your self-esteem. Each morning, I want you to get up and stand in front of the bathroom mirror. Tell yourself that you are a good person, a fun person, an attractive person. But say it with real conviction. Within a week, you'll have women buzzing all around you."

He left the office determined to follow the therapists' advice. Three weeks later, he returned with the same downtrodden expression on his face.

"Was my advice not effective?" asked the therapist.

"It worked, alright." said the man. "For the past few weeks, I've enjoyed some of the best moments in my life with the most fabulous looking women."

"So then what's your problem?" asked the therapist.

"I don't have a problem." the man replied. "My wife does."

A man was sitting on his couch watching football and drinking a beer, when his wife hit him on the head with a wooden spatula.

"What was that for? "the man asked.

The wife replied, "That was for the piece of paper with the name Jenny on it that I found in your jacket pocket!"

The man then said, "You foolish woman! When I was at the races last week, Jenny was the name of the horse I bet on."

Feeling contrite, the wife apologized and went back to folding laundry.

Three days later, the man is back on the couch avoiding the shared responsibilities of housework, when his wife bashes him on the head with a rolling pin, knocking him unconscious. Upon regaining his senses, the man demanded to know why she had hit him again.

His wife replied, "While you were sitting there watching TV, your horse phoned!"

John hoisted his beer and said, "Here's to spending the rest of me life, between the legs of me beautiful wife!" That won him the top prize at the pub for the best toast of the night!

He went home and told his wife, Mary, "I won the prize for the best toast of the night."

She said, "Aye, did ye now. And what was your toast?"

John hesitated, then said, "Here's to spending the rest of me life, sitting in church with me beautiful wife."

"Oh, that is very nice indeed, John!" Mary said.

The next day, Mary ran into one of John's drinking buddies on the street corner.

The man chuckled leeringly and said, "John won the prize the other night at the pub with a toast about you, Mary."

She said, "Aye, he told me, and I was a bit surprised myself. You know, he's only been there twice in the last four years. Once he fell asleep, and the other time I had to pull him by the ears to make him come."

An elderly couple moved to a gated community. Their new community was known for celebrating all the holidays. The old couple who hadn't celebrated Halloween in a long time, prepared to dress up and go out.

The old woman went into her bedroom, stripped naked, and tied a string around her waist. There was a lemon attached to the end of the string that dangled between her legs.

When she walked out of the room her husband yelled, "You can't go out like that!"

"This is a private gated community, I can go out dressed up as I like, and so can you!"

The man agreed and went into his room. Soon he came out naked with a string tied to his penis and a potato dangling at the end of the string. "Seriously!?!" exclaimed his wife, "That's how you're going to dress?"

"Yes," said the old man. "If you can go out as a sourpuss, I can go out as a dicktator."

After a delicious dinner and a few drinks, a wife leads her husband into the bedroom. With a very seductive voice, the woman asked her husband, "Have you ever seen $20 all crumpled up?"

"No." said her husband.

She gave him a sexy little smile, unbuttoned the top three buttons of her blouse, slowly reached down into her cleavage, and pulled out a crumpled $20 bill.

He took the crumpled $20 bill from her and smiled approvingly.

She then asked him, "Have you ever seen $50 all crumpled up?"

"No, I haven't." he said with growing anticipation. She gave him another sexy little smile. Pulled up her skirt and seductively reached into her panties and pulled out a crumpled $50 bill.

He took the crumpled $50 bill and started breathing a little quicker.

"Now," she said, "have you ever seen $50,000 all crumpled up?"

"No way!" he said while obviously becoming even more aroused and excited.

To which she replied:

"You can stay here with me or go look in the garage."

A guy goes to the supermarket and notices a beautiful woman wave at him and say hello.

He's rather taken aback because he can't place where he knows her from.

So, he responds, "I must apologize, you look very familiar, but I can't remember where I know you from?"

To which she replies, "I think you're the father of one of my kids."

Now his mind travels back to the only time he has ever been unfaithful to his wife and says, "My God, are you the stripper from my bachelor party? That night got really out of hand, and I vaguely remember having sex on the pool table with all my buddies watching."

She looks into his eyes and calmly and says, "No, I'm your son's math teacher."

A married couple is fast asleep when they are awoken by a very loud knock at the front door. The wife insists that her husband go check to see who is making such a racket. The man grudgingly puts on a housecoat and goes down the stairs to the front door. He opens it up and finds a somewhat inebriated man standing there in the dark. The man says, "Can you give me a push?"

Angry at having been woken in the middle of the night, he told the man to go away and slammed the door.

He wandered back upstairs and began to climb into his bed. His wife asked him who it was. He told her about the incident and his response. To that, she said, "Do you remember the time when we were newlyweds, we were driving in a snowstorm and got hopelessly stuck. There was that kindly man who helped push us out of the snow and we were so thankful when we got home safely that night. I think it's time to pay that back. Go downstairs and at least make sure that man gets home safely if he's drunk."

The husband grudgingly got dressed again and went downstairs. He opened his front door and called out, "Are you still out there?"

"Yes." Said the voice in the dark.

"Do you still want a push?"

"Yes." Said the voice in the dark.

"It's very dark out," said the husband, "where are you?"

"I'm on the swing set."

A woman goes into a pharmacy and approaches the pharmacist. "I would like to purchase some arsenic" she says.

"I can't sell you arsenic, it's deadly." He responds.

"I know," she says "I want to give it to my husband."

"I definitely I can't give you any arsenic, that would be homicide!" the shocked pharmacist replied. "Why would you want to give arsenic to your husband?"

"I've discovered that he's having an affair." she said as she reached into her purse and pulled out a photograph. She handed it to the pharmacist. The picture displayed her husband having sex with the pharmacists' wife.

There was an uncomfortable pause, then the pharmacist glanced again at the photo, and said, "Oh, I didn't realize you had a prescription."

A businesswoman is invited to a conference in Italy. All the travel arrangements are completed, and her husband drives her to the airport.

"Thank you honey," she says. "What would you like me to bring back for you?"

He laughs and says, "An Italian girl."

She rolls his eyes at him as any woman does who is married to a man with a tendency to say stupid things.

When the conference is over, she flies back home where her husband meets her at the airport and asks, "How was the trip honey?"

"Very good." she replies.

"And did you bring me home my present?" he asks.

"Which present?" she replies.

"The one I asked for, you know, an Italian girl."

"Oh that," she says, "Well, I did what I could. Now we must wait nine months to see if it's a girl."

A man and a woman who have never met before find themselves in the same sleeping carriage of a train.

After the initial embarrassment they both go to sleep, the woman on the top bunk, the man on the lower.

In the middle of the night the woman leans over, wakes the man and says, "I'm sorry to bother you, but I'm awfully cold and I was wondering if you could possibly get me another blanket."

The man leans out, and, with a glint in his eye and says, "I've got a better idea... just for tonight, let's pretend we're married."

The woman thinks for a moment. "Why not?" she giggles.

"Great." he replies, "Get your own bloody blanket!"

Death and Divorce

An elderly man in Phoenix calls his son in New York and says, “I hate to ruin your day son, but I have to tell you that your mother and I are divorcing; forty-five years of misery is enough.”

“Pop, what are you talking about!?!” the son screams.

“We can’t stand the sight of each other any longer.” the old man says.

“We’re sick and tired of each other, and I’m sick of talking about this, so you call your sister in Chicago and tell her.” And promptly hangs up.

Frantic, the son calls his sister, who explodes on the phone. “Like Hell they’re getting a divorce, she shouts. I’ll take care of this.”

She calls Phoenix immediately, and screams at the old man, “You are NOT getting divorced! Don’t do a single thing until I get there. I’m calling my brother back and we’ll both be there tomorrow. Until then don’t do a thing, DO YOU HEAR ME?” And she hangs up.

The old man hangs up his phone, smiles and turns to his wife. “They’re coming for Thanksgiving and paying their own way.”

It's the World Cup Final, and a man makes his way to his seat right next to the pitch. He sits down, noticing that the seat next to him is empty. He leans over and asks his neighbor if someone will be sitting there.

"No," says the neighbor. "That seat will remain empty."

"This is incredible!" said the man. "Tickets to this game are the most sought-after commodity in the sporting world. Who in their right mind would have a seat like this for the Final and not use it?"

"Well, actually the seat belongs to me. I was supposed to come with my wife, but she passed away. This is the first World Cup Final we haven't been to together since we got married."

"Oh, I'm so sorry to hear that." Said the now contrite man. "That's terrible, but couldn't you find someone else, a friend, relative or even a neighbor to take her seat?"

"No." he responded. "They're all at the funeral."

A woman was leaving a Starbucks with her morning coffee when she noticed a most unusual funeral procession approaching the nearby cemetery. A long black hearse was followed by a second long black hearse trailing about 50 feet behind. Behind the second hearse was a solitary woman walking a pit bull on a leash. Behind her were dozens of women walking single file.

Curiosity overcame her typical adherence to acceptable behavioral norms. She respectfully approached the woman walking the dog. "I am so sorry for your loss, and I know now this is a bad time to disturb you, but I've never seen a funeral like this. Whose funeral is it?"

The woman replied, "Well, that first hearse is for my husband."

"What happened to him?" the woman replied.

"My dog mistook him for an intruder in the middle of the night, attacked and killed him."

"That is horrible!" She inquired further, "Who is in the second hearse?"

The woman answered, "My mother-in-law. She was trying to help my husband when the dog turned on her."

A poignant and thoughtful moment of silence passed between the two women. "Can I borrow the dog?" she asked.

"Get in line!"

Charles Smith is on his deathbed and knows the end is near. His nurse, his wife, his daughter and two sons are with him. He asks for two witnesses to be present and a camcorder to be in place to record his last wishes. When all is ready, he begins to speak:

"My son David, I want you to take the Mayfair houses."

"My daughter Andrea, you take the apartments over in the east end." "Mark, you can have the offices over in the city center."

"Michelle, my dear wife, please take all the residential buildings on the banks of the river."

The nurse and witnesses are blown away as they did not realize his extensive holdings. And as Charles slips away the nurse says, "Mrs. Smith, your husband must have been such a hard-working man to have accumulated all this property."

Michelle replies, "Property? The asshole had a paper route."

A man places some flowers on the grave of his dearly departed mother and starts back towards his car. He notices another man kneeling at a grave. The man seems to be praying with profound intensity and keeps repeating, why did you have to die? Why did you have to die?

The first man approaches him and says, "Sir, I don't wish to interfere with your private grief, but this demonstration of pain is more than I've ever seen before. Who are you mourning? A child? A parent?"

The mourner takes a moment to collect himself, then replies, "My wife's first husband."

A husband and wife have four sons. The older three are tall with red hair and light skin while the youngest son is short with black hair and dark eyes.

The father was on his deathbed when he turned to his wife and said, "Honey, before I die, please be totally honest with me; Is our youngest son my child?"

The wife replied, "I swear on everything that is holy that he is your son."

With that assurance, the husband passed peacefully into the void.

The wife muttered under her breath, "Thank God he didn't ask about the other three."

A few days before her birthday, a husband asked his wife, "Dear, what would you like for your birthday present?"

WIFE: I really do not think you should buy me a present.

HUSBAND: How about a diamond ring?

WIFE: I don't care much for diamonds.

HUSBAND: How about a mink coat?

WIFE: You know I do not like furs.

HUSBAND: A golden necklace?

WIFE: I already have three of them.

HUSBAND: Well, Gosh, what do you want?

WIFE: What I'd really like is a divorce.

HUSBAND: Hmmm, I wasn't planning on spending that much.

Doctors and Nurses

Dr. Goldberg was a renowned physician who completed his undergraduate, medical degree and specialty training in his hometown and was then hired at the Mayo Clinic, where he quickly rose to the top of his field.

Soon he was invited to deliver a significant paper at a conference, coincidentally held in his hometown. He walked on stage and placed his papers on the lectern, but they slid off onto the floor. As he bent over to retrieve them, at precisely the wrong instant, he inadvertently farted. The microphone amplified his mistake resoundingly through the room and reverberated it down the hall. He was most embarrassed but somehow regained his composure just long enough to deliver his paper.

He ignored the thunderous applause and raced out the stage door. He immediately left his hometown and with deep embarrassment, vowed to never return again.

Many years later, when his elderly mother was ill, he could no longer avoid a homecoming. He reserved a hotel room under the name of Smith and arrived under cover of darkness. The desk clerk asked him, “Is this your first visit to our city, Mr. Smith?”

Dr. Goldberg replied, "Well, young man, no, it isn't. I grew up here and received my education here, but then I moved away."

"Haven't you visited since?" asked the desk clerk.

"Actually, I did visit once, many years ago, but an embarrassing thing happened and since then I've been too ashamed to return."

Trying his best to console him, the desk clerk replied "Sir, while I don't have your life experience, one thing I have learned is that often what seems embarrassing to me isn't even remembered by others. I bet that's also true of your circumstance."

Dr. Goldberg replied, "Son, I doubt that's the case with my incident."

The clerk asked, "Was it a long time ago?"

Dr. Goldberg replied, "Yes, many years."

The clerk asked, "Was it before or after the Goldberg Fart?"

An elderly woman goes to the doctor's office and waits for her turn to be seen. Once inside, the doctor asks what's wrong.

"I have a weird problem," she shamefully admits, "It doesn't affect anyone else, but is a minor inconvenience for me. I thought I should see you and get it checked anyway."

"Please tell me, what is your concern." replies the physician.

"I pass a lot of wind. Almost all the time. But it's okay because they are totally silent and possess no detectable odor. In fact, since coming in here I must have passed wind two dozen times, but you wouldn't have noticed."

"Hmm, interesting," pondered the doctor. "Here, take this medicine twice a day and see me in a week."

A week goes by, and the elderly woman returns for her follow-up appointment.

"What crappy medicine have you given me, you quack?!" demands the irate older lady. "My farts, although still silent, are the most fowl smelling affronts to the senses imaginable."

"Good." said the doctor. "Now that we have cleared your sinuses, let's work on your hearing."

At a trauma hospital, Doctor Jones enters a patient's room, approaches the bed and says, "Ah, I see you've regained consciousness. Now, you probably won't remember, but you were in a huge pile-up on the freeway. You're going to be okay, you'll walk again and live a pretty normal life, however, your penis was severed in the accident and we couldn't find it."

The middle aged man stared back in horror as the doctor continued, "You have $18,000 compensation coming to you through your insurance and we now have the technology to build a new penis. They work great but they don't come cheap. It's roughly $2,000 an inch."

The patient appears hopeful so, the doctor offers some advice, "You must decide how many inches you want. But understand that you have been married for over twenty-five years and this is something you should discuss with your wife. If you had a five inches before and get a nine inch replacement, she might be a bit put out. If you had a nine incher before and you decide to only invest in a five incher now, she might be disappointed. It's important that she plays a role in helping you make a decision."

The patient agrees to talk it over with his wife.

Doctor Jones comes back the next day and asks, "Have you spoken with your wife yet?"

"Yes I have," replied the patient.

"We talked about it at length. After discussing what would provide the greatest satisfaction from the insurance payout, we've decided that we're getting granite countertops."

A middle-aged man is admitted to hospital for pneumonia. A young student nurse comes into his hospital room to give him a sponge bath.

"Nurse," he mumbles from behind his mask, "are my testicles black?"

Embarrassed, the young nurse replies, "I don't know, Sir. I'm only here to wash your upper body and feet."

He struggles to ask again, "Nurse, please check for me, are my testicles black?"

Concerned that he might elevate his blood pressure and heart rate from worrying about his testicles, she overcomes her embarrassment and pulls back the covers.

She raises his gown. Holds his manhood in one hand and his testicles gently in the other.

She looks very closely and says, "There is nothing wrong with them, Sir. They look fine."

The man pulls back his oxygen mask and slowly, enunciating as well as possible given his condition, says, "Now listen very, very closely,

Are-my-test-results-back?"

An 86-year-old man went to his doctor for his quarterly check-up.

The Doctor asked him how he was feeling, and the 86-year-old said, "Things are great, and I've never felt better."

"I now have a 20-year-old bride who is pregnant with my child, so what do you think about that doc?"

The doctor considered this question for a minute and then began to tell a story.

"I have an older friend, much like you, who is an avid hunter and never misses a season."

"One day he was setting off to go hunting. In a bit of a hurry, he accidentally picked up his walking cane instead of his gun."

"As he neared a creek, he came across a very large male beaver sitting at the water's edge."

"At that moment he realized that he left his rifle at home and so he couldn't shoot the magnificent creature."

"Out of habit he raised his cane and aimed it at the animal as if it were his favorite hunting rifle and went 'bang bang'."

"Miraculously, two shots rang out and the beaver fell over dead."

"Now what do you think of that?" asked the doctor.

The 86-year-old said, "logic would strongly suggest that somebody else pumped a couple of rounds into that beaver."

The doctor replied, "My point exactly."

A man went to the hospital to visit his mother-in-law, who was gravely ill. When he returned home, his wife asked with extreme trepidation, "How's my mom doing?"

He replies: "She's doing great! She will likely still live for many years. Next week she will be released from the hospital and will come and live with us, forever!"

"Wow that's amazing!" says the wife, "But this is very strange, dear... yesterday she seemed to be on her deathbed, the doctors said she likely had only a few days to live."

"Well, I don't know how she was yesterday," he replied, "but today when I arrived at the hospital, the doctor told me that we should prepare for the worst."

A young doctor had moved to a small town to replace a doctor who was retiring.

The older doctor suggested that the young one accompany him on his rounds so that the community would become used to their new doctor.

At the first house a woman complains, “I’ve been a little sick to my stomach.”

The older doctor says, “Well, you’ve probably been overdoing the fresh fruit. Why not cut back on the amount you’ve been eating and see if that does the trick?”

As they left, the younger man said, “You didn’t even examine that woman, how did you come to your diagnosis so quickly?”

“I didn’t have to examine her. You noticed I dropped my stethoscope on the floor in there? Well, when I bent over to pick it up, I noticed a half dozen banana peels in the waste bin. I knew that was the most likely cause of her symptoms.”

The younger doctor said, “Pretty clever. If you don’t mind, I think I’ll try that at the next house.”

Arriving at the next house, they spent several minutes talking with a younger woman. She complained, “I’m feeling terribly run down lately.”

The new doctor addressed the young woman, “You’ve probably been doing too much for the Church. Perhaps you should cut back a bit and see if that helps.”

As they left, the elder doctor said, “I know that woman quite well. Your diagnosis is almost certainly correct. She’s very active in the church but how did you arrive at it?”

“I did what you did at the last house. I dropped my stethoscope and when I bent down to retrieve it, I noticed the vicar under the bed.”

A man visits his doctor to discuss the findings from his CT scan. It is a test he has now completed for the fourth time. Only the first test was required by the doctor, the next three were completed after the patient demanded the repeated tests.

“The result of your tests are conclusive,” said the doctor, “you’ve only got about six months to live.”

"There must be something I can do!" insisted the patient.

"You can have lots of mud baths." responded the doctor.

"And will that cure me?" asked the patient.

"No," replies the doctor, "but it will help you get used to lying in dirt."

A patient visits his doctor with complaints of dry skin, a dry mouth and reduced urine volume. After a thorough history and examination, the doctor says, "Take this red pill with a glass of water when you get up. Take this yellow pill with a glass of water after lunch. Take this blue pill with a glass of water after dinner and take this green pill with a glass of water at bedtime."

The patient is startled by the amount medication required to manage his condition and blurts out, "Tell it to me straight doc, what's the matter with me?"

The doctor answers, "You're not drinking enough water."

A struggling artist stops by the studio where his recent work is displayed in the gallery. The owner tells him he has good news and bad news. "The good news is that a man dropped by the studio today and put in an offer to buy every single piece. He just wanted my reassurance that art becomes more valuable after an artist passes away.

I told them they would double, possibly triple, in value. So, he bought them all."

"Wow!" exclaims the artist. "That's fantastic. What could be the bad news?"

"The guy is your doctor."

Hospital regulations require a wheelchair for patients being discharged. A student nurse found an elderly gentleman already dressed and sitting on the bed with a suitcase at his feet. He insisted that he didn't need any help to leave the hospital.

After a chat about 'rules being rules', he reluctantly allowed the young nurse to assist him into a wheelchair and pushed him towards the elevator.

On the way down she asked him if his wife was meeting him at the hospital entrance.

"I don't think so," he said. "She's still upstairs in the bathroom changing out of her hospital gown."

A seasoned medical examiner brings his new trainee to his very first crime scene. The grizzled veteran tells the rookie, "This is a messy one, are you sure you can handle it?"

The rookie says, "Of course. This is what I've been training for."

So, they go in to the room and it's a mess. All sorts of human bits and pieces are painting the floors and walls. The veteran has seen it all, so isn't fazed. He looks back at the rookie, and he seems fine. Solid as a rock. They get to the body and start uncovering the white cloth.

They uncover the head, and half of it is missing. The rookie looks unaffected.

They uncover the body, and it looks like someone used it as a piñata, viscera and blood everywhere. At this point, the rookie almost looks bored.

They uncover the legs. Muscle, tendons, and bone all blended together.

Again, no issues from the rookie as he leans in to write his notes.

They uncover the feet. The feet are fine, except one of the pinky toes has been cleanly removed.

The rookie sees this, runs out of the room, vomits uncontrollably, then passes out.

After the rookie recovers, the seasoned medical examiner addresses the now disheveled young man, "Let me guess, you're lack-toes intolerant."

Golfing, a good walk spoiled

A husband and wife are both golf fanatics. During one of their golf vacations, they play a very challenging course. They are both having great rounds until the husband hooks his drive on the 13th hole and the ball rolls up to the doorway of the greenskeeper's shed. The back of the shed is open, and he sees that if the front door is opened, he could have a shot at the green. His wife holds the door open, and he takes a full swing but misjudges his alignment. The ball strikes his wife midforehead and kills her instantly.

Years later, he had moved on with his life. He remarried and returned to the same golf course with his new wife. On the very same hole that tragedy struck, he hooked his drive again and the ball rolled up to the doorway of the greenkeeper's shed.

His new wife, an avid golfer, saw the opportunity for a miracle shot through the open doors of the shed and suggested the shot to her husband.

"NO WAY!" he replied, "I tried that shot years ago and ended up taking a triple bogie."

A foursome of lady golfers were enjoying a beautiful summer day. They arrived at the tee box of a magnificent par 5.

The first of the group teed off and was delighted by the feel of the near perfect swing and watched in awe as the golf ball arced into the clear blue sky, and then watched in horror as her ball headed directly toward a foursome of men that she had assumed were out of her range. She belatedly yelled 'FORE'.

The men turned to see where the call had come from, and the ball hit one of the men.

He immediately clasped his hands together at his groin, fell to the ground and proceeded to roll around in agony.

The woman rushed down to the man, and immediately began to apologize.

"Please allow me to help. I'm a Physical Therapist and I know I could relieve your pain if only you'd allow me." she told him.

"Oh, no, I'll be all right. I'll be fine in a few minutes." the man grunted.

He was in obvious agony, lying in the fetal position, still clasping his hands there at his groin.

At her persistence, however, he finally allowed her to help. She gently took his hands away and laid them to the side, loosened his pants and put her hands inside.

She administered tender and artful massage for several long moments until the man's labored breathing slowed and asked, "How does that feel?"

He replied, "It feels really nice, but I still think my thumb's broken."

Two guys were playing golf one day when one of them noticed a funeral procession going by on the road next to the course. He stopped in mid-swing, closed his eyes, and said a short prayer.

The other man was truly moved by this and said, "Wow! That was one of the most respectful acts I have ever witnessed. I had no idea you had that in you."

"I think it's the least I can do." the other man said, "I was married to her for 45 years."

A golfer sets his ball on the tee and lines up his shot. He takes a massive swing and puts the ball into a huge forest of trees along the fairway. He finds his ball and sees an opening. He thinks he could sneak the ball through the gap and play his ball well up the fairway. Taking out his 3-wood the golfer takes another mighty swing. The ball bounces off a tree and ricochets back at him, nailing him in the forehead and killing him instantly.

Saint Peter meets him at the pearly gates and asks how his golf game has been progressing.

The golfer said to Saint Peter confidently, "Got up here in two, didn't I?"

A young woman has been taking golf lessons and decides to play her first round.

She's just started when she gets stung by a bee.

The pain is so bad she has to go back to the clubhouse.

Her golf pro sees her come into the clubhouse and asks her, "Why are you back so early? What's the matter?"

She replies, "I was stung by a bee."

The golf pro says, "Oh no! Where?"

The woman says, "Between the first and second hole."

The pro nods knowingly and says, "Apparently your stance is too wide."

A man and a woman meet in a bar and fall madly in love. So much so, in fact, that just a week later they decide to get married.

After the ceremony, the guy says to his new bride, "I've a confession to make. I'm completely obsessed with golf. I eat, sleep, and breathe it. I hope you don't hate me for it."

The woman looks at her new husband and says, "I could never hate you, but I have a confession as well. I'm a hooker."

The man gets a pained look on his face, and after a long pause says, "Well... show me your stance."

A woman joins a country club and when she hears the guys talking about their golf round, she says, "I played on my college's golf team. I was pretty good. Mind if I join you next week?"

No one wants to say 'yes', but they're on the spot. Finally, one man says, "Okay, but we start at 6:30 AM" He figures the early tee-time will discourage her.

The woman says this may be a problem and asks if she can be up to 15 minutes late.

They roll their eyes, but say, "Okay."

She's there at 6:30 AM sharp and beats all of them with an eye-opening 2-under par round.

She's fun and pleasant and the guys are impressed. They congratulate her and invite her back the next week. She smiles, and says, "I'll be there at 6:30, or 6:45."

The next week she again shows up at 6:30 sharp. Only this time, she plays left-handed.

The three guys are incredulous as she still beats them with an even par round, despite playing with her off-hand.

They are totally impressed. She's very pleasant and a gracious winner.

They invite her back again, but each man harbors a burning desire to beat her.

The third week, she's 15 minutes late, which irritates the guys. This week she plays right-handed and narrowly beats all three of them.

The men grumble that her late arrival is petty gamesmanship on her part.

However, she's so charming and complimentary of their strong play, they can't hold a grudge.

This woman is a riddle none of the men can figure out.

They have a couple of beers in the clubhouse and finally, one of the men asks her, "How do you decide if you're going to golf right-handed or left-handed?"

The lady blushes, and grins. "When my dad taught me to play golf, I learned that I was ambidextrous." she replies. "I like to switch back and forth."

"I developed a silly habit after I got married. You see, my husband is not a golfer and I do my best not to wake him up when I have an early tee time. But just before I leave the house, I gently lift the covers off the bed. If his willie points to the right, I golf right-handed, if it points to the left, I golf left-handed."

The guys think this is hysterical.

Astonished at this bizarre information, one of the guys says, "What if it's pointing straight up?"

She says, "Then, I'm fifteen minutes late."

A husband and wife are playing golf. They're on the ninth green when the wife suddenly collapses. "Help me dear!" she groans to her husband.

So, the husband calls 911 on his cell phone, talks for a few minutes, then he picks up his putter and lines up his putt. His wife uses all her remaining strength to raise her head off the green and stares at him as she gasps, "I'm dying here and you're putting?"

"Don't worry, dear," says the husband calmly, "they found a doctor on the second hole and he's coming to help you.

"Well, how long will it take for him to get here?" she asks feebly.

"Oh no time at all," says her husband. "Everybody's already agreed to let him play through."

Police are called to an apartment. They arrive to find a woman holding a bloody 3-iron standing over a lifeless man.

The detective asks her, "Ma'am, is that your husband?"

"Yes." says the nearly catatonic woman.

"And did you hit him with that golf club?"

"Yes, yes, I did." the woman says as she begins to sob, drops the club, and puts her hands on her face.

"How many times did you hit him?"

"I don't know; put me down for a five."

A foursome of guys is waiting at the men's tee, while another foursome of women is hitting off from the ladies' tee.

The ladies are taking their time. When the final lady is ready to hit off, she hits the ball about 10 feet. She goes over to it, lines it up, takes an almighty swing and misses it completely.

Then she hacks it another 10 feet and then stands there dejectedly, quietly cursing under her breath.

She glances up at the patiently waiting men and snarls, "I guess all those fucking lessons I took over the winter didn't help one little bit!"

One of the men immediately responds, "Well, there you have it, you should've taken golfing lessons instead!"

A man staggered into a hospital with a concussion, multiple bruises, two black eyes, and a five-iron wrapped tightly around his throat.

Naturally, the Doctor asked him, "What happened to you?"

"Well, I was having a quiet round of golf with my wife, when at a difficult hole, we both sliced our golf balls into a field of cattle."

"We went to look for our golf balls. While I was looking around, I noticed one of the cows had something white at its rear end. I walked over, lifted its tail, and sure enough, there was a golf ball with my wife's monogram on it embedded right in the middle of the cow's bottom."

"Still holding the cow's tail up, I yelled to my wife, Hey, this looks like yours."

"I really don't remember much after that."

A man in his mid-twenties entered a confessional, made the sign of the cross, and announced, "Bless me Father, for I have sinned. It's been three years since my last confession."

The priest replied, "What is your sin, my child?"

"Well," the young man began, "I used profane language and I feel terrible about it."

"When did you do use this profanity?" asked the concerned priest.

"This morning, I was golfing with friends and hit an incredible drive that looked like a perfect shot that should have travelled at least 250 yards, but after covering only 100 yards it struck an electrical wire that was hanging over the fairway and fell straight to the ground."

"So that's when you swore." reasoned the priest.

"No, Father." said the young man. "After that, an Eastern Gray Squirrel scampered out of the woods, grabbed my ball in his mouth, and took off with it."

"Is that the moment when you swore, my child?"

"Well, no, Father," said the young man, "while the squirrel was running away with my ball a Red-tailed Hawk dove out of the sky, grabbed the squirrel in his talons, and started flying away."

Thinking he had figured out the reason for the young man's profanity-filled tirade, the Priest concluded, "So that's when you swore."

"No, Father," the man replied, "as the hawk carried the squirrel away in his claws, it flew towards the green and as it passed over a section of forest near the green, the squirrel dropped my ball."

"That's when you swore?" the now impatient Priest asked in a stern voice.

"No, Father, because as the ball fell it struck a tree, bounced through some bushes, careened off a big rock, rolled through a sand trap onto the green and stopped within six inches of the hole."

The frustrated Priest shook his head and in a moment of great clarity asked, "You missed the goddamned putt, didn't you?"

An attractive young woman joins three men for a round of golf. She plays the best round of her life, and the foursome arrives at the 18th hole. As they group stands on the green and begins lining up their putts, the woman realizes that if she sinks her putt, she will have the lowest score of her life. But it's a long, difficult putt with a significant hill and at least two breaks.

So excited by the prospect of shooting her best score, she asks the men for advice on her putt. She goes even further and adds, that she will give a blow job to the man who can tell her how to finish her round with just one stroke. All three men give the problem their full attention and take turns offering their opinions.

The first suggests that she should aim ten feet above the hole and hit with force to roll two feet past the cup. The second suggests aiming six feet above the hole but hitting with force to roll three feet past the cup. The third reexamines the slope of the green, turns to the attractive young woman and says, "I think it's a gimme."

Heaven, Hell and Religion

A car full of nuns is sitting at a traffic light, when a bunch of rowdy drunks pull up alongside of them.

"Hey, show us yer tits!" shouts one of the drunks.

Quite shocked, Mother Superior turns to Sister Mary and says, "I don't think they know who we are. Show them your cross."

Sister Mary rolls down her window and shouts, "Piss off ya little bastards, before I come over there and rip yer balls off!"

Sister Mary then rolls up her window, looks back at Mother Superior quite innocently, and asks, "Did that sound cross enough?"

Joe is at the pearly gates waiting to be admitted while St. Peter is leafing through his files to see if Joe is worthy of entry.

"Joe," says St. Pete, "I can't see that you've done anything really bad in your life, but I can't see that you've done anything really good that would qualify you for Heaven. Can you tell me ANY good deed you've ever done?"

Joe thinks for a moment and says, "Sure. I was driving through a bad part of town when I saw about 50 biker guys assaulting this poor girl. I slammed on my brakes, grabbed a tire iron, and walked up to this big guy who seemed to be the leader."

"As the bikers formed a circle around me, the girl took advantage of the distraction and ran away. I laid that tire iron right across the leaders' head, and he dropped like a stone."

"Then I turned and yelled to the rest of them and said, If I ever see you guys around this town again, I'll give you a real lesson in pain."

"Wow!" says St. Peter, "I guess you really do qualify for Heaven. Tell me, when did this happen?"

"Oh," says Joe, "about two minutes ago."

The Devil was sitting at the gates of Hell when an old man suddenly arrived in a burst of flames, looking confused and lost. The Devil looked at his paperwork and frowned. He was unable to find this old man's data file.

"This can't be right," the old man grumbled, looking at the Devil, "I've been a good man my whole life."

The Devil nodded apologetically, most people said this when they arrived in Hell. "Why don't you start by telling me how you died, and we'll figure it out."

The old man sighed and said, "Well, I was out minding my grandchildren and enjoying a fun day out. I don't get the grandchildren often because my eyesight is starting to fade. But we were having the most wonderful time."

"And that's when everything went crazy! Out of nowhere, I spotted the largest, most grotesque mouse I've ever seen moving towards us. It was absolutely enormous!"

"It came straight towards the grandchildren and my protective instincts took over!"

"So what did you do?" the Devil whispered, entranced by the story.

The old man continued, "You don't get how big this mouse was! Radiation must've been. Too many phones these days, that's what causes it. I did the only thing I could! I grabbed my walking stick, and I cracked it over the head. Now my eyesight isn't that good anymore, but I whacked it good!"

"The kids started screaming at this point. I guess they figured out how close they had come to being that animal's next meal."

"So you killed it?" the Devil asked. Some of his demigods had come to listen to the story.

The old man nodded, "By golly I did! There was blood splattered everywhere. The kids were crying inconsolably, and a crowd had gathered, all screaming at the sight."

"It was at this point though, that the exertion caught up with me. I felt my heart give way. I must have suffered a heart attack. Next thing I know, I'm here."

"Well..." the Devil said, concerned, "This doesn't seem to add up. Let me just give Heaven a call and we'll try and see what's going on here.

The Devil disappeared and reappeared a moment later.

"Your story checks out." the Devil said. "Must have been a mix up."

"You're all set to be taken up to Heaven. Just one question before you go. Where you were when you died?"

"Oh that's easy, I was at Disneyland."

Two guys are standing in line to enter Heaven. One turned around and asked the other how he died. "I froze to death. How about you?"

"I had a heart attack after a very stressful event." said the second man.

"If you don't mind my asking," said the first man, "what was the stressful event?"

"Well, I suspected my wife was cheating on me. So after work I went straight home. I ran upstairs to find my wife sleeping by herself. So convinced was I that she was having an affair, I ran back downstairs and looked in all the hiding spots. When I was running back up the stairs, I had a heart attack."

"That's ironic." said the first man.

"Why?" said the heart attack victim.

"If you would've looked in the fridge, we'd both be alive."

One Sunday morning, everyone in a bright beautiful tiny town got up early and went to the local church. Before the service started, the townspeople were sitting in the pews and talking about their lives, their families, and upcoming events. Suddenly there is a thunderclap and a blinding flash of light and Satan appears in the front of the church. Everyone started screaming and running for the exit, trampling each other in a frantic effort to get away from evil incarnate. Soon everyone had evacuated from the church, except for one elderly gentleman who sat calmly in his pew, not moving, seemingly oblivious to the fact that God's ultimate enemy was in his presence.

Stunned at this man's apparent lack of concern, the devil asked the man, "Do you know who I am?!?"

The man responded, "I sure do."

"So you realize that you are in the presence of pure evil and yet you are not afraid! How is that possible?"

"Well sir, I was married to your sister for 40 years."

The preacher's Sunday sermon was, "Forgive Your Enemies." Nearing the completion of the sermon, he asked, "How many in this congregation have forgiven their enemies?" About half held up their hands. He then asked, "How many of you have contemplated forgiving your enemies?" About 80 % held up their hands. Then he asked, "Having listened to this sermon, how many of you will find it in your hearts to forgive all your enemies?" All raised their hands, except one elderly lady.

"Mrs. Johnson, are you not willing to forgive your enemies?" asked the preacher.

"I don't have any," said Mrs. Johnson.

"Mrs. Johnson, that is very unusual. How old are you?"

"Ninety-three," she replied.

"Mrs. Johnson, please tell the congregation how a person can live a full life and have not an enemy in the world?"

The sweet little lady tottered down the aisle, climbed on to the dais, faced the congregation and said, "I outlived every one of those bitches!"

Three men of questionable moral fiber, died on Christmas Eve and were met by Saint Peter at the pearly gates.

"In honor of this holy season," Saint Peter said, "we have reduced the minimal requirement for entry into Heaven. To be admitted, you must each possess something that symbolizes Christmas."

The first man fumbled through his pockets and pulled out a lighter. He flicked it on. "It's a candle." he said.

"You may pass through the pearly gates." Saint Peter said.

The second man reached into his pocket and pulled out a set of keys. He shook them and said, "They're bells."

Saint Peter said, "You may pass through the pearly gates."

The third man started searching desperately through his pockets and finally pulled out a pair of women's panties.

St. Peter looked at the man with a raised eyebrow and asked, "And just what do those symbolize?"

The man replied, "These are Carol's."

The Pope is way ahead of schedule for his ride to the airport. He asks his driver if he could drive around for a while because they have time to kill, and he hasn't driven a car since becoming the Pope.

Naturally, he's a bit rusty and his driving is erratic. This draws the attention of a patrol car. The lights and siren are turned on and the officer signals for the Pope's car to pull over. When the officer comes up to the window his eyes go wide. He says to the Pope, "Hold on for a minute," and goes back to his car to radio the chief.

TRAFFIC COP: Chief we have a situation. I've pulled over an important figure.

CHIEF: How important? A governor or something?

TRAFFIC COP: No sir. He's bigger.

CHIEF: So, what? a celebrity or something?

TRAFFIC COP: More important, sir.

CHIEF: A major politician?

TRAFFIC COP: No sir, he's much more important.

CHIEF: WELL WHO IS IT!?

TRAFFIC COP: Well actually I'm not sure. But the Pope is his driver.

While teaching religion class one morning, Sister Bridget was speaking to her third-grade class and she asked, "When you die and go to Heaven, which part of your body goes first?"

Matthew stands up and says, "Your head, because it's at the top of your body."

"Very good logic." stated Sister Bridget.

Susie raised her hand and said, "I think it's your hands."

"Why do you think it's your hands Susie?" asked Sister Bridget.

Susie replied, "Because when you pray you hold your hands together in front of you and God just takes you by the hands."

"What a wonderful answer!" said the nun.

Little Johnny jumps out of his seat, and while hopping up and down says, "The feet are the first thing that goes to Heaven, and I'm certain!"

Sister Bridget, always one to encourage her students, turned to little Johnny and said, "Why would you think it would be your feet?"

Little Johnny said, "Well, I couldn't sleep last night, so I went into my parents' bedroom and saw something biblical! My mother's feet were straight up in the air, and she was yelling 'Oh God I'm coming!' We'd have lost her for sure if daddy hadn't been between her legs pinning her down."

There is an ancient convent in the outskirts of a city. The mother superior struggles to keep the old place from falling into disrepair but manages well with limited resources. One of the small private prayer rooms requires renovation and she finds enough money to purchase the materials for the job. To save money on labor, she asks two of the younger nuns to paint the room. But even the cost of replacing a nun's habit would be a financial stressor for the convent and she tells the women that they must not get even a drop of paint on their habits.

After conferring about this for a while, the two nuns decide to lock the room, strip off their habits, and paint in the nude. In the middle of the project, there comes a knock at the door.

"Who is it?" calls out one of the nuns.

"Blind man." replies a voice from the other side.

The two nuns look at each other and knowing that the room is a special place for people to spend time in private contemplation, decide that no harm can come from the letting a blind man into the room, they open the door.

"Nice tits!" says the man. "Where do you want these blinds?"

On the sixth day God turned to Archangel Gabriel and said: "Today I am going to create a land called Canada, it will be a land of outstanding natural beauty. It shall have tall, majestic mountains, beautiful sparkling lakes bountiful with bass and trout, forests full of elk and moose, high cliffs overlooking sandy beaches with an abundance of sea life, and rivers stocked with salmon."

God continued, "I shall make the land rich in oil so as to make the inhabitants prosper. I shall call these inhabitants Canadians, and they shall be known as the most friendly and kindest people on the earth."

The angel Gabriel says to God: "Wow, this Canada sounds amazing! Aren't you worried that this land will be so great that it will make the other countries jealous?"

"Not really," replied God, "just wait until I make their neighbors."

The Lord was growing increasingly frustrated with humanity. He was particularly unhappy with the loss of civility and the way humans were treating each other. He was beginning to consider a Sodom and Gomorrah situation. He decided to come down to earth and see for himself.

He assumed the form of a down-on-his-luck weary traveler who tried to hitch a ride while standing on the side of the highway.

Garbage was thrown on him, puddles were splashed on him, but most people simply sped past him without apparent recognition of his need for assistance. He was on the verge of giving up hope for humanity, and then a car pulled over and asked him where he wanted to go. He said he needed to get to a small village a long way away, and the driver graciously offered to take him there.

During the ride the driver was friendly and generous and offered what refreshments he had to the stranger. When they arrived at the destination the Lord was so overwhelmed by this stranger's generosity that he presented to him his true identity. He thanked the driver for restoring his faith in humanity and offered him a single wish.

The man was taken completely off guard and gave the first answer that came to him.

He said, "I really love driving, and I have never been to Hawaii. Could you build a bridge that I could drive all the way to those beautiful islands?"

The Lord replied, "Your request is materialistic. Think of the enormous challenges for that kind of undertaking."

"The supports required to reach the bottom of the ocean! The amount of concrete and steel it would take to build it will nearly exhaust several natural resources. I can do it, but it is hard for me to justify your desire for worldly things. Take a little more time and think of something that would honor the relationship that we have developed."

The man sat and thought about it for a long time. Finally, he looked up and said, "Lord, I wish that I could understand my wife. I want to know how she feels inside, what she's thinking when she gives me the silent treatment or when she cries. What she means when she says nothing is wrong, and how I can make her truly, truly happy."

The Lord replied, "Do you want two lanes or four lanes on that bridge?"

One day Mrs. Jones went to have a talk with the minister at the local church. "Reverend," she said, "I have a problem, my husband keeps falling asleep during your sermons. It's very embarrassing. What should I do?"

"I have an idea," said the minister, "take this hatpin with you. I will be able to tell when Mr. Jones is sleeping, and I will motion to you at specific times. When I give you the signal, you give him a good poke in the leg."

In church the following Sunday, Mr. Jones dozed off. Noticing this, the preacher put his plan to work. "And who made the ultimate sacrifice for you?" he said, nodding to Mrs. Jones.

"JESUS!", Mr. Jones cried as his wife jabbed him in his thigh with the hatpin.

"Yes, you are right, Mr. Jones." said the minister. Soon, Mr. Jones nodded off again. Again, the minister noticed. "Who is your redeemer?" he asked the congregation, motioning towards Mrs. Jones.

"GOD!" Mr. Jones cried out as he was stuck again with the hatpin.

"Right again!" said the minister, smiling.

Before long, Mr. Jones again winked off. However, this time the minister did not notice. As he picked up the tempo of his sermon, he made a few motions that Mrs. Jones mistook as signals to bayonet her husband with the hatpin again.

The minister asked, "And what did Eve say to Adam after she bore him his 99th son?"

Mrs. Jones poked her husband, who yelled, "You stick that goddamned thing in me one more time and I'll break it in half and shove it up your ass!"

"Amen," replied the congregation.

In Moscow, a soldier ran up to a nun. Out of breath he asked, "Please, may I hide under your skirt. I'll explain later!"

The nun agreed.

A moment later two Military Police ran up and asked, "Sister, have you seen a soldier?"

The nun replied, "He went that way." and pointed in a random direction.

After the MPs ran off, the soldier crawled out from under her skirt and said, "I can't thank you enough, sister. You see, I don't want to go fight in the Ukraine."

The nun said, "I understand completely."

The soldier added, "I hope I'm not being too rude, but you have a great pair of legs!"

The nun replied, "If you had looked a little higher, you would have also seen a great pair of balls, I don't want to go fight in Ukraine either!"

A man is driving down a deserted stretch of highway when he notices a sign out of the corner of his eye. It says, "Sisters of Mercy House of Prostitution 15 mi."

He assumes he had misread the sign and drives on without a second thought.

Soon, he sees another sign that says, "Sisters of Mercy House of Prostitution 8 mi.", and realizes that these signs are for real. When he drives past a third sign saying, "Sisters of Mercy House of Prostitution Next Right", his curiosity gets the better of him and he pulls into the drive.

On the far side of the parking lot is a somber stone building with a small sign next to the door saying, "Sisters of Mercy". He climbs the steps and rings the bell.

The door is answered by a nun in a long black habit who asks, "What may we do for you, my son?"

He answers, "I saw your signs along the highway and was interested in possibly doing business."

"Very well, my son. Please follow me."

He is led through many winding passages and is soon quite disoriented.

The nun stops at a closed door and tells the man, "Please knock on this door."

He does as he is told, and this door is answered by another nun in a long habit and holding a tin cup.

This nun instructs, "Please place $50 in the cup, then go through the large wooden door at the end of this hallway." He gets $50 out of his wallet and places it in the second nun's cup.

He then trots eagerly down the hall and slips through the door, pulling it shut behind him.

As the door locks behind him, he finds himself back in the parking lot facing another small sign.

The sign says "Go in Peace. You Have Just Been Screwed by the Sisters of Mercy".

Consider that Adam was a work in progress. God did some tweaking after he was first created until he was satisfied with the finished product. On that day, God approached Adam and said, "I've got some good news and some bad news. The good news is that I've got two new organs for you. One is called a brain. It will allow you to be very intelligent. You will be able to manipulate your environment and have meaningful conversations with Eve. The other organ is called the penis. It will allow you to populate this planet and make both you and Eve very happy.

Adam is very impressed, "Wow, that's great, but what's the bad news?"

God replies, "You're only getting enough blood to work one at a time."

An attractive young woman on a flight from Ireland asked the priest beside her, "Father, may I ask a favor?"

"Of course, child. What may I do for you?"

"Well, I bought my mother an expensive hair dryer for her birthday. It is unopened but exceeds the tariff limits and I'm afraid they'll confiscate it. Is there any way you could carry it through customs for me? Hide it under your robes perhaps?"

"I would love to help you, dear, but I must warn you, I will not lie."

"With your honest face, Father, no one will question you," she replied.

When they got to Customs, she let the priest go first. The official asked, "Father, do you have anything to declare?"

"From the top of my head down to my waist I have nothing to declare."

The official thought this answer strange, so asked, "And what do you have to declare from your waist to the floor?"

The priest replied, "I have a marvelous instrument designed to be used on a woman, which is, to date, unused."

Roaring with laughter, the official said, "Go ahead, Father. Next please!"

An Irish boy goes to confession and tells the priest he has been with a girl of loose morals.

"That's a grievous sin," the priest says, "tell me, was it Mary O'Hara?"

"No, Father."

"Was it Kate Murphy?"

"No Father."

"Was it Kathleen McGonigle?"

"No, Father. I don't want to say who it was."

Later, as the boy leaves the church, he sees a friend, who asks him, "How'd it go?"

He answers, "Well, I got ten Hail Marys, five Our Fathers and three great leads."

A pastor asks if anyone in the congregation would like to express thanks for prayers answered.

Susie Smith stands, walks to the podium, and says, "Two months ago my husband, Tom, had a terrible bicycle accident and his scrotum was completely crushed. The pain was excruciating, and the doctors didn't know if they could help him."

You could hear a mumbled gasp from the men in the congregation.

"We prayed as the doctors performed a delicate operation, and it turned out they were able to piece together the crushed remnants of Tom's scrotum and wrap wire around it to hold it in place."

All the men cringe at the thought of the pain.

The pastor rises and tentatively and asks if anyone else has something to say.

A man stands up, walks slowly to the podium, and says, "I'm Tom Smith."

The entire congregation holds its breath.

"I just want to tell my wife the word is pronounced 'sternum.'"

Three couples are meeting with their pastor to discuss joining the leadership team.

The pastor told them that to be part of the leadership team, they must learn sacrifice. He asked that they demonstrate this important quality by forgoing sexual intimacy for one month.

The three couples share awkward glances, but agree, and close the meeting in prayer.

The month passes, and they all return to the pastor's office. The pastor addresses the first couple, both in their mid-50's, "How did your month go?"

They clasp each other's hand and smile, "No problem really. We haven't had regular intercourse for quite some time and so our sacrifice was small but meaningful to us."

"Welcome to the leadership team." The pastor replied. Then he turned to the next couple, both in their 30's.

They gave a slight smile, "The first two weeks went ok. The third week was a little rougher. By the fourth week we were sleeping in separate rooms and taking cold showers, but we succeeded."

"Desires of the flesh can be strong, but your willpower remained stronger. Welcome to our leadership team."

Turning to the last couple, newlyweds in their 20's. "How was your month?"

They hung their heads in shame.

"We didn't even make it one week. The second day, I saw my wife bending over a frozen turkey and I lost all my control. I raised her dress and with wild abandon me made passionate love on that very spot."

"Well, I'm sorry," the pastor sadly responded, "but we can't allow you onto our leadership team."

The young couple slowly nodded their understanding and the wife meekly replied, "We understand. They won't let us back into Walmart either."

One Easter Sunday, a man goes to church and returns home with two black eyes.

His wife, who was feeling under the weather and stayed home, inquired as to how he got the black eyes.

The man goes on to say, "A lady stood up in front of me during Mass. I saw her dress was stuck in her butt crack, so I reached out and tugged it out. She whirled around, furious, and punched me in the eye."

"That explains one black eye," the wife says, "but what about the other?"

The man explains, "I figured she must have liked her dress stuck up in her butt crack, so when she turned around, I stuffed it back up there."

A man took his wife and his mother-in-law on vacation to Jerusalem. His mother-in-law complained incessantly. To her, the food was horrible, the accommodation was dirty, the bed was uncomfortable, and her son-in-law was too cheap to allow her to travel in comfort. She never missed an opportunity to berate her son-in-law. During the vacation, she worked herself into such a frenzied state that she had a heart attack and died. The undertaker told the husband, "You can have her shipped home for $5,000, or you can bury her here, in the Holy Land, for $500."

The man thought about it and told the undertaker he would just have her shipped home. The undertaker asked, "Why would you spend $5,000 to ship your mother-in-law home, when it would be wonderful to be buried in the Holy Land and you would only spend $500."

The man replied, "A long time ago a man died here, was buried here, and three days later he rose from the dead. I just can't take that chance."

There was an old priest who became increasingly concerned by the large number of people in his parish who kept confessing to adultery.

One Sunday, on the pulpit, he said, if I hear one more person confess to adultery, I'll quit!

Well, everyone liked him, so they came up with a codeword.

Someone who had committed adultery would say they had "fallen".

This seemed to satisfy the old priest. Years went by. Eventually the ancient priest passed away peacefully in his sleep.

The town received a new priest, fresh from the Seminary. About a week after the new priest arrived, he visited the mayor of the town and expressed his concern.

The priest said, you have to do something about the sidewalks in this town. When people come into the confessional, they keep talking about having fallen.

The mayor started to laugh, realizing that no one had told the new priest about the codeword.

Before the mayor could explain, the priest shook an accusing finger at the mayor and said I don't know what you're laughing about, your wife fell three times this week.

Law Enforcement

A police officer attempts to stop a car for speeding and the guy gradually increases his speed until he's topping 100 mph. The man eventually realizes he can't escape and finally pulls over.

The cop approaches the car and says, "It's been a long day, and my shift is almost over, if you can give me a good excuse for your behavior, I'll let you go."

The guy thinks for a few seconds and then says, "My wife ran away with a cop about a week ago. I thought you might be that officer trying to give her back!"

A man was called in for an audit by Revenue Canada. He asked his accountant for advice on what to wear.

"Wear your worst clothing and an old pair of shoes. Let them think you are a pauper." the accountant replied.

Then he asked his lawyer the same question but got the opposite advice. "Don't let them intimidate you. Wear your best suit and an expensive tie."

Confused, the man went to his minister, told him of the conflicting advice, and asked him what he should do.

"Let me tell you a story." replied the minister. "A woman about to be married asked her mother what to wear on her wedding night. Her mother told her to wear a heavy long flannel nightgown that goes right up to the neck and wool socks. But when she asked her best friend, she got conflicting advice. Her friend told her to wear her most sexy negligée with a V-neck right down to her navel."

The man protested, "But reverend, what does all this have to do with my problem with Revenue Canada?"

The Reverend replied, "It doesn't matter what you wear, you're still going to get screwed."

An old farmer got up in the middle of the night to use the toilet.

As he was heading back to bed, he looked out the window and saw the lights on in his shed. A closer inspection revealed men loading his tools and farm machinery into their truck.

He rushed to the phone and called 911.

"I need the police! There are some guys clearing out my shed!"

"OK sir, we have dispatched officers, they should be there in about an hour."

"An hour?! But they'll be long gone by then!"

"I'm sorry sir but there are no officers in your area."

The farmer hangs up angrily, waits 10 minutes and then calls 911 again.

"Hi, it's me again. Don't worry about sending those cops, I've just shot the robbers." and he hangs up.

Less than 10 minutes later, three cop cars and a helicopter arrive and the robbers are arrested. The sergeant goes up to the house and bangs on the door. The farmer opens the door and is standing there wearing his dressing gown and holding a cup of tea.

"What's going on here!? You said you shot the robbers!" shouted the sergeant.

Without a hint of remorse, the farmer replied, "And your department said there were no officers in my area."

A Texas patrolman pulls over a car for speeding. Inside are two young men heavily tattooed, shaven heads and the kind of physiques that can only be created by using huge doses of testosterone. The driver rolls down his window and the patrolman hits him across the face with his flashlight.

"Ow! What was that for?" asks the driver.

The patrolman replies, "In Texas, drivers have their license and registration ready when I come to the window." He writes the driver a ticket and gives it to him. Before the driver can roll up the window, he is hit again with the flashlight.

"Ow!" yells the driver, "What the hell was that for?"

"In Texas, when we give you a ticket, you say thank you." Replied the patrolman.

The driver quickly says thank you and rolls up the window.

The patrolman then walks around to the passenger side of the car and taps on the window. The passenger rolls down his window and is immediately struck on the head with the flashlight.

The passenger yells, "Ouch! Why the hell did you do that?"

The Patrolman responds, "I was making your wish come true."

"What wish?" demanded the passenger.

The patrolman responds, "In one minute you would have turned to your buddy and said, I wish that son of a bitch had tried that shit with me."

The IRS suspected a fishing boat owner wasn't paying proper wages to his deckhand and sent an agent to investigate him.

IRS AUDITOR: I need a list of your employees and how much you pay them.

BOAT OWNER: Well, there's Clarence, my deckhand, he's been with me for three years. I pay him $1,000 a week plus free room and board. Then there's the mentally challenged guy. He works about 18 hours every day and does about 90% of the work around here. He makes about $10 per week, pays his own room and board, and I buy him a bottle of Bacardi rum and a dozen Budweisers every Saturday night so he can cope with life. He also gets to sleep with my wife occasionally.

IRS AUDITOR: That's the guy I want to talk to, the mentally challenged one.

BOAT OWNER: That would be me. What would you like to know?

A game warden catches an unlicensed fisherman in the act. "You're going to pay a big fine for all those fish in your bucket."

"But officer, I didn't catch these." said the fisherman. "They are my pet fish and I just bring them here to swim. When they're done, they jump back into the bucket."

"Oh really? This I've got to see. If you can prove it, I'll let you go."

The fisherman empties the bucket into the lake and waits patiently. A few minutes go by, and nothing happens.

The Game warden asks, "So where are the fish?"

The Fisherman responds, "What fish?"

A Highway Patrolman waited outside a popular bar, anticipating an easy arrest of a drunk driver. Just before closing time, a man staggered out of the bar. The man could barely remain upright, he was most certainly inebriated. He stumbled around the parking lot for a few minutes, looking for his car. He finally found his car and climbed in as the bar closed and the patrons began to leave.

He sat in the car for a good ten minutes. He turned his lights on, then off, wipers on, then off. He started to pull forward onto the grass, then stopped.

Finally, when he was the last car in the parking lot, he pulled out onto the road and started to drive away. The patrolman, waiting for this, turned on his lights and pulled the man over. He administered the breathalyzer test, and to his great surprise, the man blew a zero. The patrolman was dumbfounded. "This equipment must be broken!" He exclaimed.

"I doubt it," said the man, "tonight I am the DD."

The patrolman looked at him with confusion, "I don't see how you could be the designated driver when you are stumbling drunk."

"No," said the man, "I'm the designated decoy!"

On the first day of a trial for a horrendous double-homicide the judge takes his seat, and the defendant is asked to remain standing.

The Judge says to him "You've been charged with beating your wife to death with a hammer."

A voice in the back of the courtroom yells out "YOU BASTARD!"

The Judge bangs his gavel to quiet the court then continues "You are also charged with beating your mother-in-law to death with a hammer."

The same voice in the back of the courtroom yells "YOU ROTTEN BASTARD!"

The Judge glares towards the back of the courtroom and announces, "Sir, I can understand your anger and outrage at these crimes, but please refrain from any more outbursts or I will have to have you removed from my court!"

The man stands and says, "I'm sorry your honor, but for fifteen years I have lived next door to that asshole and every time I asked him if I could borrow a hammer, he said he didn't have one!"

In court, the trucking company's lawyer was questioning Clyde. "Didn't you say, just after the accident, 'I'm fine.'" asked the lawyer?

Clyde responded, "Well, I'll tell you what happened. I had just loaded my favorite mule, Bessie, into the..."

"I did not ask you for any details," the lawyer interrupted. "Just answer the question. Did you not say, at the scene of the accident, 'I'm fine?'"

Clyde said, "Well, I had just got Bessie into the trailer, and I was driving down the road."

The lawyer interrupted again and said "Judge, I'm trying to establish the fact that, at the scene of the accident, this man told the highway patrolman on the scene that he was just fine. Now several weeks after the accident he is trying to sue my client. I believe he is a fraud. Please tell him to simply answer the question."

By this time the judge was fairly interested in Clyde's answer and said to the lawyer, "I'd like to hear what he has to say about his favorite mule, Bessie."

Clyde thanked the judge and proceeded.

"Well as I was saying, I had just loaded Bessie, my favorite mule, into the trailer and was driving down the highway, when this huge semi-truck and trailer ran the stop sign and smacked my truck right in the side. I was thrown into one ditch and Bessie was thrown into the other. I was hurting real bad and didn't want to move. However, I could hear old Bessie moaning and groaning. I knew she was in terrible shape just by her groans.

When the highway patrolman came on the scene, he could hear Bessie moaning and groaning so he went over to her. After he looked at her and saw her near fatal condition, he took out his gun and shot her between the eyes."

"Then the patrolman came across the road, gun still in hand, looked at me and said, 'How are you feeling?'"

"Now what the hell would you say?"

Lawyers, my favorite target

A man was bemoaning his fate after the meeting with his ex-wife and her lawyer where they completed the documents for their divorce. The terms of the settlement would leave him with very little.

As he aimlessly strolled through the back streets of his seaside town, he came across a small antiques shop. In the window was a life size statue of a golden rat standing on its back legs with one paw raised like it was about to say something profound. He went inside and said to the owner, "How much for the statue of the rat in the window?"

The owner said, "That is an interesting piece, and it comes with quite a story. I can sell you the statue for $250, but if you want the story, you'll have to pay $500."

The guy considers, then hands the owner $250. The owner hands over the statue and says, "You'll be back."

The guy takes his statue and walks out. As he heads up the street, he hears a scratching behind him and looks back. There in the street, in broad daylight, is a rat following him. Odd, he thinks and keeps going. After about 100 meters he looks back and now there are half a dozen rats. Unusual!

He goes a bit further and now there are dozens of rats, and he starts to get worried. He picks up his pace and looks back. Now there are scores of rats, so he starts to run. Every now and then he looks back and it is getting worse and worse.

Hundreds of rats, thousands, all running after him. He screams and runs headlong through the town, down to the sea and all the while these rats are following. So he starts to wade out into the ocean. Out to his knees, his waist, his chest and the rats keep coming, so he throws the statue of the golden rat as far as he can out to sea, and the rats all swim past him to where the statue sank. They follow the statue down and are never seen again.

He wades back to the shore, wet, miserable, and bedraggled. He heads back up through the town to the antiques shop. He opens the door and walks inside. The owner of the shop looks up and grins at the soaking wet man and says, "I knew you'd be back. Have you come to pay me the extra $250 for the story?"

The man says no. "I was wondering if you had a statue of a lawyer."

A young man is waiting in line at the post office when he notices an older man in the corner of the office licking stamps that say 'Love' on them and putting them on bright pink envelopes.

The man then takes a bottle of perfume from his jacket pocket and sprays the envelopes. Curiosity gets the better of the young man, so he walks over and asks the older man what he is doing.

"I'm sending out 500 Valentines' cards with the phrase guess who? written inside."

"Why?" the younger man asks.

The man smiles and says, "Because I'm a divorce lawyer."

In a small town, a United Way volunteer worker noticed that the most successful lawyer in the whole town hadn't made a single contribution. This guy was making about $600,000 a year, so the volunteer thought, why not call him up?

"Sir, according to our research you haven't made a contribution to the United Way, would you like to do so?"

The lawyer responds, "A contribution? Does your research show that I have an invalid mother who requires expensive surgery once a year just to stay alive?"

The worker is feeling a bit embarrassed and says, "Well, no sir, I'm..."

"Does your research show that my sister's husband was killed in a car accident? She has three kids and no means of support!"

The worker is feeling quite embarrassed at this point. "I'm terribly sorry..."

"Does your research show that my brother broke his neck on the job and now requires a full-time nurse to have any kind of normal life?"

The worker is completely humiliated at this point. "I am sorry sir, please forgive me..."

"The audacity of you people! If I don't give them anything, why should I give it to you!"

A Mafia Godfather finds out that his bookkeeper, Guido, has cheated him out of 10 million dollars. The bookkeeper is deaf. That was the reason he got the job in the first place. It was assumed that Guido would hear nothing so he would not have to testify in court regarding conversations he had overheard within the organization.

When the Godfather goes to confront Guido about his missing money, he takes along his lawyer who knows sign language.

The Godfather tells the lawyer, "Ask him where the money is?"

The lawyer, using sign language, asks Guido, "Where's the money?"

Guido signs back, "I don't know what you are talking about."

The lawyer tells the Godfather, "He says he doesn't know what you are talking about."

The Godfather pulls out a pistol, puts it to Guido's temple and says, "Ask him again!"

The lawyer signs to Guido, "He'll kill you if you don't tell him."

Guido signs back, "OK. Just tell him not to shoot me. The money is in a brown briefcase, buried behind the shed at my Cousin Bruno's house."

The Godfather asks the lawyer, "What did he say?"

The lawyer replies, "He says you don't have the balls to pull the trigger."

A wealthy lawyer is driving down the road in his limo when he sees two men eating grass on the side of the road. He pulls over to investigate.

He asks the men, "Why are you eating this disgusting grass?"

The men reply, "We're too poor, it's all we have."

The lawyer replies, "You and your buddy can come home with me, and I'll feed you."

The man replies, "But sir, we both have families."

The lawyer replies, "Bring them all!" And they all pile into the car.

One of the men's wives turns to the lawyer and tells him, "Thank you so much sir, we really needed this."

The lawyer responds, "No problem, the grass is almost a foot tall, you'll love it!"

A man charged with assault and battery insisted at his trial that he had just pushed his victim 'a little bit'. When he was pressured by the prosecutor to demonstrate just how hard it was, the defendant refused on their grounds that he would not give the lawyer an opportunity to harass him for another insignificant assault. The lawyer, thinking that he could entrap the defendant, turned to the judge, "Your honor, if I promise not to press charges, would you allow the defendant to provide a demonstration?"

To which the judge said he would allow it.

The defendant then approached the lawyer, slapped him in the face, grabbed him firmly by the lapels, and flung him over the table and across the room.

He then faced judge and jury, and calmly declared, "I would say it was about one-tenth as hard as that."

A New York attorney representing a wealthy art collector called his client and said to him, "Saul, I have some good news and I have some bad news."

The art collector replied, "I've had an awful day, let's hear the good news first."

The attorney said, "Well, I met with your wife today, and she informed me that she invested $5,000 in two pictures that she thinks will bring a minimum of $15-20 million. I think she could be right."

Saul replied enthusiastically, "Well done! My wife is a brilliant businesswoman! You've just made my day. Now I know I can handle the bad news. What is it?"

The attorney replied, "The pictures are of you with your secretary."

An ambitious lawyer is alone in his office daydreaming about schemes to advance his career when Satan suddenly appears before him and says, "I am aware of your deepest desires and am here to offer you a deal. You will become the most successful attorney who has ever lived. You will be rich beyond imagination and known to everyone on the planet. You will be appointed to the Supreme Court, and your rulings will be read and studied for decades to come. All I ask for in return, is the souls of your wife and your three children."

The lawyer sits with his head in his hands, thinking for several minutes. Finally, he says, "Okay, what's the catch?"

A man goes out drinking with his buddies most Friday nights. His buddies often meet young ladies and leave the bar with them. This man, however, has no luck at all and always goes home alone. He is tired of his lack of success and asks one of his buddies for advice.

His buddy asks him to recount the conversations he has with the women he meets in the bars.

He explains that most of the encounters begin with typical small talk, and things seem to go smoothly.

Eventually he lets them know that he is an accountant, and shortly after that the conversation seems to lose momentum.

"Well, that's it!" exclaimed his buddy. "You tell a woman in a bar that you are an accountant, and they think small, cramped offices, spread sheets and calculators. They assume that you are boring. Instead, what you should do is tell them that you are a lawyer. They will think about court rooms and drama and will find you way more interesting."

So, the next time they are out, he begins a conversation with a good-looking young woman and before long, tells her that he is a lawyer. She becomes very interested in him and after a couple of drinks, they leave the bar together and go back to her apartment.

They have a couple more drinks at her apartment and before long they end up in bed.

They have an intimate encounter and when it is over the man lies back in the bed and starts to laugh out loud. The woman asks why he is laughing, and he responds:

"I've only been a lawyer for a couple hours and already I've screwed somebody."

A lawyer dies, and somehow manages to go to Heaven. When he gets there, he's greeted by St. Peter himself. The lawyer says, "What happened? I wasn't in an accident and I'm too young to die. I'm only 52!"

St. Peter says, "Nope, by our records, you are 84, and that's a pretty good life."

The lawyer yells, "84! How did you figure that?"

St. Peter responds, "We added up your client billing time sheets."

There is a trial in a small southern town in the United States, and the prosecuting attorney calls his first witness, the small town's matriarch. He approached her and asked, "Mrs. Jones, do you know me?"

She responds, "Why, yes, I do know you, Mr. Williams. I've known you since you were a boy, and frankly, you've been a big disappointment to me. You lie, you cheat on your wife, you manipulate people and talk about them behind their backs. You think you're a big shot when you haven't the brains to realize you'll never amount to anything more than a two-bit paper pusher. Yes, I know you."

The lawyer was stunned. Not knowing what else to do, he pointed across the room and asked, "Mrs. Jones, do you know the defence attorney?"

She again replied, "Why yes, I do. I've known Mr. Bradley since he was a youngster, too. He's lazy, bigoted, and he has a drinking problem. He can't build a normal relationship with anyone, and his law practice is one of the worst in the entire state. Not to mention he cheated on his wife with three different women. One of them was your wife. Yes, I know him." The defense attorney nearly died.

The judge asked both counselors to approach the bench and, in a very quiet voice, said,

"If either of you idiots asks her if she knows me, I'll send you both to the electric chair."

At a convention of pharmaceutical researchers, the presenters review their latest discoveries and advances in their field. One presenter tells the audience that his lab is making tremendous progress with their experiments which he credits to having switched from rats to lawyers for their test subjects.

"At first we weren't sure why this should be so effective, so we commissioned a study."

"The study identified three reasons for this unprecedented improvement and one qualification statement."

"First, we found that lawyers are far more plentiful than rats. Second, the lab assistants don't get so attached to them. And third there are some things even a rat won't do."

"The proviso is, that it is very hard to extrapolate our test results to human beings."

For three years, the young attorney had been taking his brief vacations at a small country inn. The last time he'd been there, he finally managed to have an affair with the innkeeper's beautiful daughter. Looking forward to an exciting few days, he dragged his suitcase up the stairs of the inn, then stopped short. There sat his lover with an infant on her lap!

"Helen, why didn't you write when you learned you were pregnant?" he cried. "I would have rushed up here, we could have gotten married, and the baby would have my name!"

"Well," she said, "when my folks found out about my condition, we sat up all night talkin' and talkin' and decided it would be better to have a bastard in the family than a lawyer."

A group of terrorists burst into the conference room at the Ramada Hotel, where the American Bar Association was holding its annual convention. More than a hundred lawyers were taken as hostages.

The situation was very intense. The hotel lobby became filled with military and the media was accumulating in the parking lot. Finally, the specially trained negotiator arrives on the scene. The terrorist leader uses a megaphone and loudly declares, "Give us ten million dollars and safe passage to a country that does not have an extradition agreement." He goes on further to say, "If our demands are not met, we will release one lawyer every hour."

Respect Your Elders

A couple, both age 76, went to a sex therapist's office. The doctor asked, "What can I do for you?"

The man said, "Will you watch us have sexual intercourse?" The doctor looked puzzled but agreed.

When the couple finished, the doctor said, "There's nothing wrong with the way you have intercourse," and charged them $80.

This happened several weeks in a row. The couple would make an appointment, have intercourse with no problems, pay the doctor, then leave.

Finally, the doctor asked, "Just exactly what are you trying to find out?"

The old man said, "We're not trying to find out anything. She's married and we can't go to her house, I'm married, and we can't go to my house. The Holiday Inn charges $120; the Hilton charges $150. We do it here for $80 and I get $64 back from my health plan."

An elderly couple noticed that they were getting a lot more forgetful. They went to see their doctor for some advice. The doctor told them that they should start writing things down, to offset their failing memory.

That evening, while sitting together on the sofa watching a show, the elderly wife asked her husband to get her a bowl of ice cream. "You might want to write it down," she said.

The husband said, "No, I can remember that you want a bowl of ice cream."

She then added, "Please put some chocolate sauce on top of the ice cream. You should write that down," she told him.

Again, he said, "No, no, I can remember, you want a bowl of ice cream with chocolate sauce."

A thought occurred to the old woman, and she said, "and a cherry on top. Write it down!"

Again, he said, "No, I got it. You want a bowl of ice cream with chocolate sauce and a cherry on top." So, he goes to get the ice cream and spends an unusually long time in the kitchen, over 30 minutes. He comes back and hands his wife a plate of bacon and eggs.

His wife stares at the plate for a moment, then looks at her husband and asks, "Where's the toast?"

A husband notices his wife's hearing is deteriorating and decides to visit his doctor for advice.

"What can I do for my wife if she is losing her hearing?" asked the elderly man.

"How bad is her hearing loss?" asked the doctor.

She refuses to have it tested and I don't know how to measure her hearing," replied the frustrated old man.

"There's a simple trick you can use to gauge her hearing loss," explains the doctor. "Simply ask her a question at a distance and if she doesn't hear you, move closer and ask again until she does."

That evening, after a round of golf with his buddies, the husband arrives home and sees his wife in the kitchen cooking. He thinks to himself, 'what a perfect opportunity to test her hearing.'

As he stands in the entrance hallway of their home, in a normal speaking volume, he says, "Hi honey, I'm home. What's for dinner?"

No answer. He moves to the kitchen entrance. "Hi honey, I'm home. What's for dinner?"

Still no answer. He moves halfway across the kitchen. "Hi honey, I'm home. What's for dinner?"

Still his wife doesn't answer. He now sees how serious her hearing problem is. At this point, he is standing right behind his wife and says, "Hi honey, I'm home. What's for dinner?"

"FOR THE FOURTH BLOODY TIME WE'RE HAVING CHICKEN!"

A few old couples enjoy getting together once a week for a shared meal and to talk about life. One day, while the ladies were busy in the kitchen, one of the men, Harry, started talking about a fantastic restaurant he had gone to the previous night with his wife.

He thought the food was excellent and felt he could recommend the place to his friends.

"What's the name of the restaurant?" one of the men asked. After thinking for a few seconds, Harry said, "What are those good smelling flowers called again?"

"Do you mean a rose?" the first man offered.

"Yes, that's it," he exclaimed. Looking over towards his wife in the kitchen, he shouted, "Rose, what's the name of that restaurant we went to the other night?"

An 85-year-old man marries a 25-year-old woman. Given the difference in their ages, they agree to have separate rooms in their married life to reduce the potential health risks for the older man.

On their wedding day, after the nuptials, they go to their new home together and head to their respective rooms to prepare for bed.

Several minutes later, the young bride hears the expected knock at the door and welcomes in her new husband for the anticipated consummation of their marriage. The old man performs well and after the love making kisses his new bride goodnight and heads back to his room.

Fifteen minutes later the young bride is surprised by another knock at her door and when she answers, she finds her new husband standing there with a smile on his face and a bulge in his night robe. She happily invited him in and again they made love as newlyweds should. Afterwards, he again kissed her good night and retired to his room.

About fifteen minutes later, there was another knock at the young bride's door. And you guessed it, the old man was back and raring to go. They made love again and afterwards the young woman turned to her new husband and said, "Your stamina is amazing! I have been with men one third your age who can only make love once a night and you have done it three times!"

The old man appears quite embarrassed and answers, "You mean I was here already?"

Three elderly men are sitting together and discussing what they want their family and friends to say when they are lying in their casket at their funeral.

The first man says, "I want them to say I was a great father and a great friend. I want them to say I could always be counted on."

The second guy says, "I just want them to talk about how much I changed the world, and how I left it a better place."

The third man says, "I want them to observe me very closely and say, 'Look! He's moving!'"

Three senior citizens are sitting on a park bench complaining about their failing bodies.

"Every morning, I get up at six AM," the first man explains, "and I try to pee, but only a trickle comes out."

The second man adds, "I get up at six AM also, and it feels like I've got to move my bowels, but I sit down on the toilet, and nothing happens." The third man chimes in on the conversation and tells his friends, "I pee and move my bowels at exactly seven AM every morning."

"That's not bad," the first man responds. "Why are you complaining?"

The third man explains, "The problem is I don't usually wake up until eight AM."

In a long-term care residence, a very busy nurse is doing her best to look after numerous residents. As she is walking down the hallway, she sees Mr. Smith coming towards her and notices that he appears very sad. She asks him what's the matter?

He answers, "Today my penis died."

The nurse is quite accustomed to looking after confused residents and so she offered her condolences and went about her business.

The next day, while walking down that same hallway, she sees Mr. Smith, coming towards her with his penis dangling through his unzipped pants. "Mr. Smith, you can't walk down the hallway with your private parts showing. You need to put that back inside of your pants!" The nurse exclaimed.

Mr. Smith looks at her with a very long face and replied, "Yesterday I told you that my penis died. Today is the viewing."

An 80-year-old man who had been treated for prostate cancer agreed to be in a medical study regarding the effects of the treatment. As a part of the study, he was required to do a semen analysis.

The doctor gave the man a specimen jar and said, "Take this home and bring back a semen sample tomorrow."

The next day the 80-year-old man reappeared at the doctor's office and gave him the specimen jar which was as clean and empty as on the previous day.

The doctor asked what happened and the man explained, "Well, doc, it's like this, first I tried with my right hand, but nothing. Then I tried with my left hand, but still nothing. Then I asked my wife for help. She tried with her right hand, then with her left, still nothing. She tried with her mouth, first with the teeth in, then with her teeth out, still nothing."

"We even called up Irene, the lady next door and she tried too, first with both hands, and even tried squeezin' it between her knees, but still nothing."

The doctor was shocked! "You asked your neighbor?"

The old man replied, "Yep, but none of us could get the jar open."

My neighbor is a 90-year-old with Alzheimer's who lost his wife over 20 years ago.

I see him every morning when I open my front door to retrieve the newspaper.

At each of these encounters, the poor old man asks me If I've seen his wife.

This could be heartbreaking and make one consider moving, but when I tell him the truth, the look of joy in his eyes is priceless.

Frank is 85 and lives in a senior citizens home. Every night after dinner he goes to a secluded garden behind the home to sit and ponder his accomplishments and long life. One evening, Mildred, age 82, wanders into the garden. They begin to chat and before they know it, several hours have passed.

After a short lull in their conversation, Frank turns to Mildred and asks, "Do you know what I miss most of all?"

"What?" she asks.

"Sex." he replies

Mildred exclaims, "Why you old toot. You couldn't get it up if I held a gun to your head!"

"I know," Frank says, "but it would be nice if a woman could just hold it for a while."

"Well, I can oblige," says Mildred, who unzips his trousers, removes his manhood and proceeds to hold it.

Afterward, they agree to meet secretly each night in the garden where they would sit and talk, and Mildred would gently grasp Frank's penis. Both elders seemed happy with this arrangement which went on for weeks. Then one night Frank didn't show up at their usual meeting place

Alarmed and fearing the worst, Mildred went in search of her dear friend. Her anxiety increased when she found that he was not in his room. With growing anxiety, she hurried through the common rooms. She eventually wandered out to the pool where she found him sitting on a deck chair with Ethel, another female resident, who was holding Frank's little pal!

Furious, Mildred yelled, "You two-timing son-of-a-bitch! What does Ethel have that I don't have?"

Old Frank smiled happily and replied, "Parkinson's."

The doctor that had been seeing an 80-year-old woman for most of her life, finally retired.

At her next checkup, her new doctor told her to bring a list of all the medicines that had been prescribed for her.

As the young doctor was looking through these, his eyes grew wide as he realized she had a prescription for birth control pills.

"Mrs. Smith, do you realize these are birth control pills?"

"Yes, they help me to sleep at night."

"Mrs. Smith, I assure you there is absolutely nothing in these pills that could possibly help you sleep!"

She reached out and patted the young Doctors' knee.

"Every morning, I grind up one of the pills and mix it in a glass of orange juice that my 16-year-old granddaughter drinks, and believe me, it helps me sleep at night."

Four elderly men are sitting together on a park bench. They meet regularly and enjoy drinking coffee as they discuss the news and share stories about their glory days. They argue and debate over everything. On this day they are offering their opinions about the fastest thing that exists. The first man insists that thoughts are the fastest as they just 'pop' into your head. The second man is certain that a blink is faster as in the saying, "in the blink of an eye".

The third old man says you're both wrong. "When I flick a light switch, the light comes on instantaneously."

The three men who have provided their opinions look to the fourth man awaiting his judgment. After a moment, he looks at all three men and states, "You're all wrong. The fastest thing that exists is diarrhea!"

The three men stare in disbelief and demand that he explain himself.

The fourth man responded, "Yesterday I awoke with a horrible sensation in my belly, before I could think, blink or turn on the light, I shit the bed!"

An elderly couple had just learned how to send text messages on their cell phones.

The wife was a romantic type, and the husband was more of a no-nonsense guy.

One afternoon the wife went out to meet a friend for coffee. She decided to send her husband a romantic text message and she wrote:

If you are sleeping, send me your dreams.
If you are laughing, send me your smile.
If you are eating, send me a bite.
If you are drinking, send me a sip.
If you are crying, send me your tears. I love you.

The husband texted back to her:

I'm on the toilet. Please advise.

Technology and Education

The graduate with a science degree asks, "Why does it work?"

The graduate with an engineering degree asks, "How does it work?"

The graduate with an accounting degree asks, "How much will it cost?"

The graduate with a sociology degree asks,

"Do you want fries with that?"

A lawyer is having difficulty logging into his company's high security network and calls the IT department for assistance. The tech support worker meets him at his computer terminal and asks the lawyer to demonstrate the problem.

As the lawyer starts typing, the tech grows increasingly curious. He notices that the sign-in seems overly complex. He asks the lawyer what password he is using to access the system. The lawyer replies, DocGrumpyHappySleepyBashfulSneezyDopeySnowwhiteRome

The tech support worker is shocked and asks why he chose such a long password.

To which the lawyer responded, "Well the instructions were to have a password with eight characters and at least one capital."

A middle-aged married man is having trouble with erectile dysfunction.

He had tried all the conventional treatments without any real measure of success.

He heard about a medicine man who lived just on the edge of the desert and was rumored to have a very good treatment for this problem.

Having given up on modern medicine, he set out to find this Shaman to see if he possessed a solution to his problem.

He found the old man living in the traditional manner of his ancestors.

After describing his problem. The old man handed a potion to him, and with a grip on his shoulder, warned, "This is a powerful medicine. You take only a single teaspoon and then say 1-2-3."

"When you do, you will become more manly than you have ever been in your entire life, and you can perform for as long as you want."

The man was encouraged and as he walked away, he turned and asked, "How do I stop the medicine from working?"

"Your partner must say 1-2-3-4." The Medicine man responded. "But when she does, the medicine will not work again until two full moons have passed."

The man was very eager to see if it worked, so he went home, showered, shaved, took a spoonful of the medicine. He then invited his wife to join him in the bedroom.

When she came in, he quickly stripped off his clothes and said, "1-2-3."

Immediately he was the manliest of men.

His wife was excited and began throwing off her clothes and while doing this she asked, "What was the 1-2-3 for?"

And that, ladies and gentlemen, is why you should never end your sentences with a preposition. If you do, you could end up with a dangling participle.

A professor, known for his difficult exams, handed out the test papers for the semester finals. He started the timer.

When time ran out, he collected the completed tests. The professor noticed that one of the students had attached a $100 bill to his test with a note saying, "A dollar per point."

The next class the professor handed the graded tests back. That student got his graded test back and $52 change.

George received a text message:

> Hi, George. This is Richard, next door. I've a confession to make. I've been riddled with guilt for a few months and have been trying to get up the courage to tell you face-to-face. At least I'm telling you in this text.
>
> I can't live with myself a minute longer without your knowing about this. The truth is, when you're not around, I've been sharing your wife, day and night. Probably much more than you. I haven't been getting it at home recently. I know that's no excuse. The temptation was just too great. I can't live with the guilt and hope you'll accept my sincere apology and forgive me.
>
> Please suggest a fee for usage and I'll pay you. Richard

George, feeling enraged and betrayed, grabbed his gun, went next door, and shot Richard dead. He returned home, shot his wife, poured himself a stiff drink and sat down on the sofa.

George then looked at his phone and discovered a second text message from Richard.

> Hi, George. Richard here again. Sorry about the typo on my last text. I assume you figured it out and noticed that the darned autocorrect changed 'Wi-Fi' to 'wife'. Technology, huh? It'll be the death of us all.

The following is an actual bonus question given on a university chemistry mid-term exam.

Is Hell exothermic (gives off heat) or endothermic (absorbs heat)?

Most of the students wrote proofs of their beliefs using Boyle's Law (gas cools when it expands and heats when it is compressed) or some variant.

One student, however, wrote the following:

First, we need to know how the mass of Hell is changing over time. We need to know the rate at which souls are moving into Hell and the rate at which they are leaving. I think that we can safely assume that once a soul gets to Hell, it will not leave. Therefore, no souls are leaving. As for how many souls are entering Hell, let's look at the different religions that exist in the world today.

Most of these religions state that if you are not a member of their religion, you will go to Hell. Since there is more than one of these religions, and since people do not belong to more than one religion, we can project that all souls go to Hell. With birth and death rates as they are, we can expect the number of souls in Hell to increase exponentially.

Now, we look at the rate of change of the volume in Hell because Boyle's Law states that in order for the temperature and pressure in Hell to stay the same, the volume of Hell has to expand proportionately as souls are added.

This gives two possibilities:

If Hell is expanding at a slower rate than the rate at which souls enter Hell, then the temperature and pressure in Hell will increase until all Hell breaks loose.

If Hell is expanding at a rate faster than the increase of souls in Hell, then the temperature and pressure will drop until Hell freezes over.

So, which is it? If we accept the postulate given to me by Teresa during my Freshman year at university, that, 'It will be a cold day in Hell before I sleep with you,' and take into account the fact that I slept with her last night, then number two must be true, and thus I am sure that Hell is exothermic and has already frozen over. The corollary of this theory is that since Hell has frozen over, it follows that it is not accepting any more souls and is therefore, extinct, leaving only Heaven, thereby proving the existence of a divine being, which explains why, last night, Teresa kept shouting 'Oh my God.'

The Working Man

I work for a large financial institution. The staff parking lot is enormous, and it takes me five minutes to walk from my parking spot to the office. One morning, as I was completing that long journey, I saw the CEO of my company getting out of his Ferrari which he parked in his reserved spot right beside the office building. He saw me looking admiringly at his expensive sports car, and he said to me, "If you work hard for this company, if you put in overtime without asking compensation, if you truly believe you can make a difference and instill the same passion into your colleagues...

... then probably next year I'll be able to afford a Lamborghini."

A guy goes to an employment office to apply for a job. They ask him, "Do you have allergies?"

He says, "Yes, caffeine, I can't drink coffee."

"Okay, have you ever been in the military?"

"Yes." he replies, "I was in Iraq for one tour of duty."

The interviewer says, "That will make you a strong candidate!" Then he asks, "Are you disabled?"

The guy says "Yes, a bomb exploded near me and blew off both testicles."

The interviewer grimaces, "Okay, that puts you over the top and I can hire you right now. Our normal hours are from eight AM to four PM every day. You start tomorrow, be here every day starting at ten AM."

The guy is puzzled and asks. "If the work hours are from eight AM to four PM, why don't you want me here until ten AM every day?"

"This is a government job", the interviewer says, "for the first two hours we sit around drinking coffee and scratching our balls, no point in you coming in for that."

Upon arriving home, a husband was met at the door by his sobbing wife. Tearfully she explained, "It's the pharmacist. He insulted me terribly this morning on the phone. I had to call multiple times before he would even answer."

Immediately, the husband drove downtown to confront the pharmacist, and demand an apology.

Before he could say more than a word or two, the pharmacist told him:

"Now, just a minute, listen to my side of it. This morning my alarm failed to go off, so I was late getting up. I went without breakfast and hurried out to the car, just to realize that I'd locked the house with both house and car keys inside and had to break a window to get my keys."

"Then, in an attempt to make up lost time, I drove too fast and got a speeding ticket. When I was about three blocks from the store, I got a flat tire."

"When I finally got to the store a bunch of people were waiting for me to open up. I got the store opened and started waiting on these people, all the time the darn phone was ringing."

He continued, "Then I had to break a roll of coins against the cash register drawer to make change. The coins spilled all over the floor. I had to get down on my hands and knees to pick them up and the phone was still ringing. When I stood up, I cracked my head on the open cash drawer, which made me stagger back against a showcase with a bunch of perfume bottles on it. Half of them hit the floor and broke. Meanwhile, the phone is still ringing with no let up, and I finally got back to answer it. It was your wife. She wanted to know how to use a rectal thermometer!"

"Sir, as God is my witness, all I did was tell her!"

Three engineers and three accountants are traveling by train to a conference. At the station, the three accountants each buy tickets and watch as the three engineers buy only a single ticket.

"How are three people going to travel on only one ticket?" asks an accountant.

"Watch and you'll see." answers an engineer.

All of them board the train. The accountants take their respective seats but all three engineers cram into a restroom and close the door behind them. Shortly after the train has departed, the conductor comes around collecting tickets. He knocks on the restroom door and says, "Ticket, please."

The door opens just a crack, and a single arm emerges with a ticket in hand. The conductor takes it and moves on. The accountants saw this and agreed it was a clever idea.

So, after the conference, the accountants decide to copy the engineers on the return trip and save some money.

When they get to the station, they buy a single ticket for the return trip. To their astonishment, the engineers don't buy a ticket at all.

"How are you going to travel without a ticket?" says one perplexed accountant.

"Watch and you'll see." answers an engineer.

When they board the train the three accountants cram into a restroom and the three engineers cram into another one nearby. The train departs. Shortly afterward, one of the engineers leaves his restroom and walks over to the restroom where the accountants are hiding. He knocks on the door and says, "Ticket, please."

Three contractors are bidding on a contract to fix a broken fence at the White House. All three go with a White House official to examine the fence.

The first contractor takes out a tape measure and does some measuring, then works some figures with a pencil. "Well," he says, "I figure the job will run $8,000. The breakdown is $3,500 for materials, $3,500 for my crew, and $1,000 profit for me."

The second contractor also does some measuring and figuring, then says, "I can do this job for $7,000. That's $3,000 for materials, $3,000 for my crew, and $1,000 profit for me."

The third contractor doesn't measure or figure but leans over to the White House official and whispers, "$9,000."

The official, incredulous, says, "You didn't even measure like the other guys! How did you come up with such a high figure?"

He leans in even closer and whispers back, "$1000 for me, $1000 for you, and we hire the other guy to fix the fence for $7,000."

A farmer living by a country road is increasingly concerned by speeding traffic. Worried that he and his livestock are in danger, he calls the police and asks them to put up a sign. They put up a 'Slow' sign, but it has no effect. They tried putting up a 'Pedestrian crossing' sign but that had no effect either. Finally, they tried erecting a 'Children at play' sign, but the traffic still kept whizzing past. Eventually the farmer asks if he can put up his own sign and the police agree. A few days later a policeman stops by to see how things are going. He's amazed to see the traffic moving at a snail's pace, then he notices the farmer's homemade sign, it read, 'Nudist Colony.'

A university graduate is applying for a part-time job to help with his course fees. He applies to work in a supermarket and gets the job. The first day, the manager tells him to sweep the floor.

The University grad is furious and shouts, "Hey, don't you know that I have several degrees in various areas of science, and after seven years of going to university, you ask me to sweep the floor?!?"

The manager replied, "Oh sorry, I didn't know that, here pass me the broom and I'll show you how to sweep the floor."

A philosopher, a mathematician, and a physicist were in a Starbucks.

The mathematician turns to the physicist standing next to him and says, "You know, physics is just applied mathematics!" They have a good laugh, at which point the philosopher interjects from across the counter. "And mathematics is just applied philosophy!"

Everyone has a good laugh, and then the physicist turns to the philosopher and says,

"Now shut your trap and make my coffee."

A woman takes her dog to the vet to treat a skin condition causing the dogs' fur to become thickly matted.

"Don't worry." The vet offers, "there is a prescription ointment that works well for this problem."

When the woman finds out that the treatment is quite expensive, she asks the vet if he can make out the script in her name so that she can use her extended health coverage to pay for the ointment. He reluctantly agrees.

She drops the prescription at the pharmacy and returns later that day to pick up the medication. The pharmacist reviews the use of the treatment and provides the appropriate warnings. "You'll have to be very careful when you apply this ointment. If it's for your underarms, make sure you don't use any deodorant for at least two days, otherwise you'll get a huge rash."

She responds, "Ah, but it's for" and as she hesitates the pharmacist tries to help her out adding, "Well, if it's for your legs, make sure you don't wear any tights for at least three days!"

"No, no," says the woman, "you don't understand. It's for my Schnauzer." She says sheepishly.

"In that case," he says, "you'd better not ride a bike for at least a week!"

Juan was the best oyster diver in his small seaside village. One day he found an injured sea otter and nursed it back to health. From the moment the grateful otter was able to walk, it never left Juan's side. It even learned to dive for oysters and to bring his catch back to Juan. Their combined oyster harvest was so successful that he developed a reputation all along the coast.

One day, a man arrived at Juan's house looking to hire him for a week.

His wife answered the door. "Sure," his wife said. "It will cost you $500."

"That much?" replied the prospective client.

"But you're getting my husband and his otter. They can harvest more oysters than anyone else in town."

"I just want Juan. I'll hire him alone for $350." the man countered.

"Sorry," she shrugged. "You can't have Juan without the otter."

A Swedish farming village in the middle ages is facing a crisis. They haven't had any rain in almost two months. Most of their crops are dead or dying, and many of the citizens are starving.

One day, Sven comes bursting into his kitchen, scooping his wife Helga into his arms and dancing with joy.

"Sven! What's gotten into you? Why are you so happy?" Helga asks.

"My darling. I've just spoken to Rudolph." Sven replies. "You know Rudolph. He's got a great plait of fire red hair and a big, bushy red beard! He says that we'll get four inches of glorious rain by tomorrow! Oh joy, all our problems are solved!"

Helga slaps her husband. "Oh Sven! You've gotten my hopes up. Why are you so confident in this Rudolph fellow?"

Sven beams at his wife and says, "Because Rudolph the Red knows rain, dear!"

A man was driving along a country road when he noticed a chicken running alongside his car. He was amazed to see the chicken keeping up with him, as he was doing 50 kph. He accelerated to 60, and the chicken stayed right next to him. He sped up to 75 kph, but the chicken overtook him.

Then the man noticed that the chicken had three legs. So surprised was he that he followed the chicken, speeding all the way, and ending up at a farm. He got out of his car and saw that all the chickens on the farm had three legs.

When he spotted the farmer he asked him, "Where did you get these chickens?"

The farmer replied "Well, everybody likes chicken legs, so I figured that I could increase my profit per chicken if I could breed a three-legged bird. And after multiple attempts I was finally successful! I'm going to be a millionaire!"

The man was impressed and asked him how they tasted.

The farmer said, "Don't know, I haven't caught one yet."

A wealthy married woman is approached by her maid who politely requests a substantial raise in her meager wages.

The lady of the house has a reputation of being tight with her money and demands to know why her servant should be entitled to such a significant raise.

The maid responds, "Well Ma'am, there are three reasons why I deserve an increase. The first is that I iron better than you do."

"Who said that you iron better than me?" asked the wealthy woman.

"Your husband said so." replied the maid. And she went on, "The second reason is that I am a better cook than you."

"Nonsense!" said the woman. "Who said you were a better cook than I am?"

"Your husband did."

The wealthy woman was becoming increasingly agitated.

"And the third reason," said the maid, "is that I am better at sex than you are."

The wife is seething now, and through gritted teeth, demands, "And did my husband say that as well?"

"No Ma'am." answered the maid, "the gardener did."

"Oh, ok! So, how much do you want?"

One evening an old farmer wanders down to his pond to confirm that the water level was adequate for the remainder of the season. He hadn't been there in months. As he got closer, he heard loud giggling coming from the pond. He was shocked to find a bunch of young women skinny-dipping. "Hey what's going on here?" he shouted, alerting the women who were standing at the waters' edge.

The women screamed in shock and swam to the deep end of the pond. One of the women shouts back at the farmer, "We're not coming out until you leave you pervert!"

The old man replies, "I didn't come down here to watch you ladies swim or see you naked! I'm here to feed the alligators."

A very wealthy couple was going out for the evening. The lady of the house spoke to their butler before they left. She said, "Jeeves why don't you take the night off? I think we will not be home until quite late."

As it turned out, the wife was not having a good time at the party, so she came home early.

She walked into the house and saw Jeeves sitting alone in the dining room.

She called for him to follow her. She led him into the master bedroom.

She closed and locked the door.

She looked at him and smiled. "Jeeves," she said, "Take off my dress."

He did so carefully.

"Jeeves," she said, "Take off my bra." He silently obeyed her.

"Jeeves," she said, "Remove my panties." The tension mounted as he complied.

Finally, she looked at him and said, "Jeeves, if I ever catch you wearing my clothes again, you're fired."

A photographer from a well-known national magazine was assigned to cover the fires at Yellowstone national Park.

When the photographer arrived, he realized that the smoke was so thick that it would seriously impede or make it impossible for him to photograph anything from ground level. He requested permission to rent a plane and take photos from the air.

He arrived at the airport and saw a plane warming up near the gate. He jumped in with his bag and shouted, "Let's go!"

The pilot swung the little plane into the wind, and within minutes they were in the air.

The photographer said, "Fly over the park and make two or three low passes so I can take some pictures."

"Why?" asked the pilot.

"Because I am a photographer, he responded, and photographers take photographs."

The pilot was silent for a moment, finally he stammered, "You mean you're not the flight instructor?"

There is a factory in northern Minnesota which makes the Tickle-Me-Elmo toys. The toy laughs when you tickle it under the arms.

Lena is hired at the Tickle-Me-Elmo factory, and she reports for her first day promptly at eight o'clock in the morning.

The next day at 8:45 there was a knock at the personnel manager's door. The foreman throws open the door and begins to rant about the new employee. He complains that she is incredibly slow and the whole line is backing up, putting the entire production line behind schedule.

The personnel manager decides he should see this for himself, so the two men march down to the factory floor. When they get there the line is really backed up. There are Tickle-Me-Elmos all over the factory floor and they're beginning to pile up. At the end of the line stands Lena surrounded by mountains of Tickle-Me-Elmos. She has a roll of plush red fabric and a huge bag of small marbles. The two men watched in amazement as she cut a little piece of fabric, wrapped it around two marbles and began to carefully sew the little package between Elmo's legs.

The Personnel manager bursts into laughter. After several minutes of hysterics, he pulls himself together and approaches Lena.

"I'm sorry," he says to her barely able to keep a straight face, "but I think you misunderstood the instructions I gave you yesterday, your job is to give each Elmo two test tickles."

Odds & Ends

A family is at the dinner table. The son asks his father, "Dad, how many kinds of boobs are there?"

The father, surprised, answers, "Well, son, a woman's boobs go through three phases. In her 20s, a woman's boobs are like melons, round and firm. In Her 30s to 40s, they are like pears, still nice but hanging a bit. After 50, they are like onions."

"Onions?" Replied the young man.

"Yes, you see them, and they make you cry."

This infuriated his wife and daughter, so the daughter said, "Mom, how many kinds of willies are there?"

The mother, surprised, smiles and answers, "Well dear, a man's willie goes through three phases also. In his 20s, his willy is like an oak tree, mighty and hard. In his 30s and 40s, it is like a birch, flexible but reliable. After his 50s, it is like a Christmas tree."

"A Christmas tree?" asks the daughter.

"Yes—dead from the roots up and the balls are just ornamental."

Joe smiled all the time. He was very old and despite his age, continued the rigorous, nomadic life of a working cowboy. One evening, while sitting at the campfire, a younger man, relatively new to this grueling lifestyle, asked Old Joe for his secret to living such a long and happy life.

Joe responded in a gravelly drawl, "There are five things you must do. Find a woman who can make you laugh, find a woman who can cook, find a woman who really listens to you, find a woman who is amazing in bed, and lastly, and most importantly, cuz your happiness and longevity are dependent on it, make sure these four women never meet."

Cinderella wants to go to the ball, but her wicked stepmother won't let her. As Cinderella sits crying in the garden, her fairy godmother appears and promises to provide Cinderella with everything she needs to go to the ball, but with two important conditions. "First, you must wear a diaphragm."

Cinderella agrees. "What's the second condition?"

"You must be home by 2 AM. Any later and your diaphragm will turn into a pumpkin."

Cinderella agrees to be home by 2 AM.

The appointed hour comes and goes, and Cinderella doesn't show up.

Finally, at 5 AM., Cinderella shows up, looking love-struck and very satisfied.

"Where have you been?" demanded the fairy godmother. "Your diaphragm was supposed to turn into a pumpkin three hours ago!!!"

"I met a prince, Fairy Godmother. He took care of everything."

"I know of no prince with that kind of power! Tell me his name!"

"I can't remember, exactly… Peter Peter, something or other…"

A man visits his dentist to examine his sore tooth. The dentist does the exam and tells the man that the tooth will have to be pulled. He warns the man that the procedure will be painful and prepares to numb the area. As the dentist is preparing the injection the man begins to panic and tells the dentist that he is deathly afraid of needles and will not consent to having the freezing.

"How about laughing gas?" asks the dentist.

"Does it need to be administered with a mask?" responded the man. "Because I am horribly claustrophobic and cannot tolerate anything covering my face.

The dentist begins to lose his patience and asks, Are you ok with taking pills?"

The man replies, "I am fine with pills."

The dentist rummages through his drawer and hands the patient a pill.

"What is this?" asks the man.

"It's Viagra." Responds the dentist.

The patient says, "Wow – I didn't know Viagra worked as a pain killer!"

"It doesn't," said the dentist, "But it will give you something to hold onto when I pull out your tooth."

After 10 years, a wife started to think their child looked kinda strange, so she did a DNA test and found out the child was not theirs.

With extreme trepidation, she told her husband what she found out.

The husband replied, "You don't remember, do you? When we were leaving the hospital, the baby pooped. You told me, go and change him. So I went back into the hospital, got a clean one and left the dirty one there."

Shortly after a jumbo jet had reached its cruising altitude, the captain announced:

"Ladies and Gentlemen, this is your Captain. Welcome to Flight 293, non-stop from London Heathrow to New York John F. Kennedy. The weather ahead is good, so we should have a smooth uneventful flight.

So, sit back, relax and... OH, SHIT!"

Silence followed!

Some moments later the captain came back on the intercom. "Ladies and gentlemen, I'm sorry if I alarmed you. While I was talking to you, a flight attendant accidentally spilled a cup of hot coffee on my lap. You should see the front of my pants!"

One of the passengers yelled back, "You should see the back of mine!"

It was the final of the Olympic wrestling competition, and it had boiled down to two of the very best in the sport, Tommy, from the USA on one side, and 'The Russian Bear' on the other. The coach pulls Tommy aside for his final pre-match instructions.

"Tommy, you watch yourself out there. This Bear is a beast. He has never been beaten and whatever you do, do not let him get you into the pretzel. It is excruciatingly painful and what's more, virtually impossible to get out of. That's his signature move and how he has won four of his last five matches. Go out there and do America proud, young man."

So, out trots Tommy onto the mat where he meets this huge yeti of a man, as wide as he is tall.

The referee signals for them to get underway and the two athletes start circling each other, eying each other up for weaknesses, then BOOM, the Russian dives on top of Tommy and the crowd gasps in sympathy for the guy as they watch the

Bear twist and bend his limbs into the pretzel position. The coach looks ashen and can't watch his prized athlete be subjected to such torture and so he turns away, covering his eyes.

In the next moment, the crowd roars and the coach turns around just in time to see the Russian Bear fly up high into the air and come crashing down, hard. Tommy crawls over to the immobile figure and flops on top of him to end the match.

After the fight, the coach says, "Tommy, that was great work but, I have to be honest with you, when he got you into that pretzel, I had to look away and I never saw how you got out. How on earth did you do it?"

Tommy answered, "Well, you were right about the pretzel. It is by far the most painful thing I have ever experienced. I was starting to pass out with pain, and I really couldn't move, but I opened my eyes and looked up, I saw a pair of balls just dangling inches from my face, so I stretch out my neck as far as I could and with all the might I could summon, I bit those balls. You would be surprised how strong you become when you bite your own balls!"

Jane, Sue and Mary haven't seen each other since leaving school. They rediscover each other via a reunion website and arrange to meet for lunch in a wine bar.

Jane arrives first, wearing Versace and orders a bottle of Pinot Grigio. Sue arrives shortly afterward, in grey Chanel followed by Mary wearing a faded old tee shirt, ripped blue jeans and well-worn boots.

They begin drinking wine and sharing details of their lives since graduation.

Jane completed a master's degree at Princeton, where she met and married her husband who is now a partner at a leading law firm. They own a vacation home in Hawaii.

Sue relates that she got an MBA and worked in banking where she met her husband who is a leading investment banker. They have a yacht in Florida.

Mary explains that she left school at 17 and ran off with her boyfriend, Jim. They run a tropical bird park and grow their own vegetables. Jim can stand five parrots, side by side, on his penis.

Halfway down the third bottle of wine and several hours later, Jane blurts out that her husband is really a cashier at Walmart, and they live in a small apartment.

Sue, chastened and encouraged by her old friend's honesty, explains that she and her husband are both nurses in a retirement home and live in a basement suite.

Mary admits that the fifth parrot has to stand on one leg.

I was walking down the street when I was accosted by a particularly dirty and shabby-looking homeless man who asked me for a couple of dollars for dinner.

I took out my wallet, extracted ten dollars and asked, "If I give you this money, will you buy some beer with it instead of dinner?"

"No, I had to stop drinking years ago" the homeless man replied.

"Will you use it to go fishing instead of buying food?" I asked.

"No, I don't waste time fishing." the homeless man said. "I need to spend all my time trying to stay alive."

"Will you spend this on hunting equipment?" I asked.

"Are you NUTS!" replied the homeless man. "I haven't gone hunting in 20 years!"

"Well," I said, "I'm not going to give you money. Instead, I'm going to take you home for a shower and a terrific dinner cooked by my wife."

The homeless man was astounded. "Won't your wife be furious with you for doing that?"

I replied, "Don't worry about that. It's important for her to see what a man looks like after he has given up drinking, fishing and hunting."

There was a pirate captain who would ask his lieutenant to bring his red jacket whenever a potential enemy vessel was sighted.

One day his lieutenant asked him "Captain, why do you always wear your red jacket whenever we see a ship on the horizon?"

To which the old ruffian replied, "So that if we get into a battle, and if my enemy's sword pierces my flesh, my blood stains will not discourage the crew and thus surely we will attain victory."

One day a hundred enemy vessels were spotted approaching the pirate ship and unimaginable bloodshed was inevitable. "Lieutenant!" Cried the captain, "Bring me my brown trousers!"

A man boarded an airplane and took his seat. As he settled in, he glanced up and saw the most beautiful woman boarding the plane. He made a silent prayer to whatever gods were listening that the woman would sit nearby. As fate would have it, she took the seat right beside him.

Eager to strike up a conversation, he blurted out, "Business trip or pleasure."

She turned, smiled, and said," Business. I am a psychologist and the keynote speaker at the annual convention for the study of nymphomaniacs."

Struggling to maintain his composure, with a slight quiver in his voice, he asked, "How do you become an expert in this area of study."

"I have done extensive research in this area. I also use information that I have learned from my personal experiences.

My recent work debunks some of the popular myths about sexuality."

"Really," he said, "and what kind of myths are there?"

"Well," she explained, "one popular myth is that African American men are the most well-endowed, when in fact it is the Native American Indian who is most likely to possess that trait. Another popular myth is that Frenchmen are the best lovers when actually it is men of Jewish descent who are the best. I have also discovered that the lover with absolutely the best stamina is the southern redneck."

The woman became a little uncomfortable and blushed. "I'm sorry, she said I shouldn't really be discussing all of this with you. I don't even know your name."

"Tonto," the man said, "Tonto Goldstein, but my friends call me Bubba."

Late one afternoon, the Air Force folks out at Area 51 were very surprised to see a Cessna landing at their "secret" base. They immediately impounded the aircraft and hauled the pilot into an interrogation room.

The pilot's story was that he took off from Vegas, got lost, and spotted the base just as he was about to run out of fuel.

A thorough FBI background check was done on the pilot while he was held overnight.

By the next day, they were finally convinced that the pilot really was lost and wasn't a spy. They fueled up his airplane, gave him a terrifying "you-did-not-see-a-base" briefing, complete with threats of spending the rest of his life in prison, gave him a flight plan to return to Vegas, and sent him on his way.

The day after that though, to the total disbelief of the Air Force, the same Cessna showed up again. Once again, the MP's surrounded the plane... only this time there were two people on board.

The same pilot jumped out and said, "Do anything you want to me, but my wife is in the plane, and you have to tell her where I was last night!"

Rob and Peter plan a weekend ski trip. They loaded up Rob's minivan and headed towards the mountains.

After driving for a few hours, they got caught in a terrible blizzard. They pulled into a nearby farm and asked the lady who answered the door if they could spend the night.

"I realize it's terrible weather out there," she said, "and I have this huge house all to myself. But I'm recently widowed and I'm afraid the neighbors will talk if I let you stay in my house."

"No need to put yourself in an awkward position." Rob said. "We'll be happy to sleep in the barn, and if the weather breaks, we'll be gone at first light."

The lady agreed and the two men found their way to the barn and settled in for the night.

Come morning, the weather had cleared, and they got on their way. They enjoyed a great weekend of skiing.

But about nine months later, Rob got an unexpected letter from an attorney. It took him a few minutes to figure it out, but he finally determined that it was from the attorney of the widow he had met on the ski weekend.

He dropped in on his friend Peter and asked, "Peter do you remember the widow from the farm we stayed at on our ski holiday up north about nine months ago?"

"Yes, I do." said Peter.

"Did you uhhh, happen to get up in the middle of the night? Go up to the house and pay her a visit?"

"Well, yes." Peter said embarrassed about being found out. "I have to admit that I did."

"And did you happen to give her my name instead of telling her your name?"

Peter's face turned beet red, and he said, "Yeah, look, I'm sorry buddy, I'm afraid I did. Why do you ask?"

She just died and left me everything.

Too Short for Cement-Time

(but too funny to exclude from the book)

A woman in labor suddenly shouted, "Shouldn't! Wouldn't! Couldn't! Didn't! Can't!"

"Don't worry," said the doctor, "those are just contractions."

There's a fine line between a numerator and a denominator.

Only a fraction of people will get this joke.

What's the difference between a hippo and a zippo?

One is really heavy and the other's a little lighter.

What do you get when you cross a dyslexic, an insomniac, and an agnostic?

Someone who lies awake at night wondering if there really is a dog.

I was really embarrassed when my wife caught me playing with my son's train set by myself. In a moment of panic, I threw a bed sheet over it.

I think I managed to cover my tracks.

A pirate goes to the doctor to have the moles on his back examined. When the doctor is finished, he tells the pirate "You're okay, they're benign."

The pirate responds "Check again doc, there be at least twelve of them."

I was horrified when my wife told me that my six-year-old son wasn't actually mine. Apparently, I need to pay more attention during school pick-up.

I got an e-mail saying, "At Google Earth, we can read maps backwards!" and I thought... "That's just spam."

An elderly man went to his doctor and said, "Doc, I think I'm developing dementia. Several times lately, after going to pee, I have forgotten to zip up."

"I wouldn't be too worried about that." replied the doctor. "Dementia is when you go pee and forget to unzip."

I phoned the wife earlier and asked if she wanted me to pick up Fish and Chips on the way home, but she just grunted at me.

I think she still regrets letting me name the twins.

The first time I got a universal remote control, I thought to myself, "This changes everything."

The guy who sat next to me on the train pulled out a photo of his wife on his phone, and said, "She's beautiful, isn't she?"

I said, "If you think she's beautiful, you should see my girlfriend mate."

He said, "Why? Is she a stunner?"

I said, "No, she's an optician."

My friend keeps saying, "Cheer up man, it could be worse. You could be stuck underground in a hole full of water."

I know he means well.

What's the difference between 'kissing-ass' and 'brown-nosing'?

Depth perception.

A chicken and an egg are lying in bed. The chicken is smoking a cigarette with a satisfied smile on its face.

The egg is frowning and looking very annoyed. The egg mutters to no one in particular,

"Well, I guess we answered THAT question!"

What's the difference between ignorance and apathy?

I don't know and I don't care.

The easiest time to add insult to injury is when you are signing someone's cast.

A man is with his wife on his deathbed. He leans towards her, "Honey, I have one last wish. After I die, marry Joe."

She replies, "I thought you hated Joe?"

He looks deeply into her eyes and with his dying breath, says, "I do."

Two men are talking about how they want to leave the world. I'd like to go out like my uncle, says the first man. He died at the racetrack. The second man says he'd like to go out like his grandfather, he just died peacefully. Fell asleep and never woke up and never made a sound. Not at all like the people riding in his bus.

A man told his doctor he wasn't able to do all the things around the house that his wife expected him to do. When the examination was complete, the man said, "Tell me in plain English Doc, what's wrong with me?"

"Well, in plain English," the doctor replied, "you're just lazy."

"OK," said the man, "now give me the medical term so I can tell my wife."

When I was at the grocery store, I asked an employee where the cereal was, and he said, "I'll see." And walked off. Five minutes later, I asked another employee about the cereal, and he too said, "I'll see," and walked off.

I eventually found it myself. It was in aisle C.

The sky was looking ominous, so I asked Siri, "Surely, it's not going to rain today?"

And she replied, "Yes, it is, and don't call me Shirley."

That was when I realized I'd left my phone on Airplane mode.

I heard of a book where Pavlov's dog and Schrodinger's cat have a cross-country adventure. When I asked the librarian about it, she said, "It rings a bell, but I'll have to check whether it's there or not."

At a funeral for an old biology professor, a man walks up to the widow and asks if he can speak at the service. The widow readily accepts his offer.

During the service the man walks up to the podium leans into the microphone and says the single word 'plethora'. He then steps away from the podium and walks over to the widow.

"Thanks," she says, "that means a lot."

Best friends are sitting on the front porch, drinking a beer and reminiscing about old times. Bob turns to Mark and says, "It was exactly 20 years today! I remember it like it was yesterday. You came running out of that room, tears rolling down your face, yelling it's a boy! It's a boy!"

"And since that day, we have not returned to Thailand."

I discovered my mother-in-law has weekly sessions with Lucifer himself on how to be even more vicious.

I've no idea what kind of fees she's charging him.

A couple is sitting on their porch, relaxing and sipping wine. The wife says, "I love you."

The husband says, "Is that you or the wine talking?

The wife replies, "It's me, talking to the wine."

What's the difference between a Catfish and a Lawyer?

One's a bottom dwelling scum sucker and the other one's a fish.

I tried donating blood today… NEVER AGAIN! Too many stupid questions:

Whose blood is it? Where did you get it from? Why is it in a bucket?

A Prescription For Laughter

The first edition of this book generated a surprising number of questions exploring the connections between humor and medicine. This led me to reflect upon humorous patient interactions I have experienced during my 35 years in general practice. There is a treasure trove of material and I've chosen three stories to demonstrate the power of laughter in the medical setting.

As men age, prostate health becomes a concern and leads to the infamous digital rectal exam (DRE). Understandably, most men approach this procedure with anxiety, and over-compensate with the usual one-liners. While initially amusing, the same silly quips have lost their charm over time. So, in the twilight of my career, I've challenged my patients to up the ante and try to make me laugh.

I recall explaining this to 'Ross', one of my patients due for his complete physical. "Before your DRE, please do not ask 'Will you still respect me in the morning?' Do not ask me to dim the lights, and no, I will not take you out for dinner first."

Entering the exam room, I found Ross fully clothed and grinning at me conspiratorially. There was a paper bag beside him on the exam table.

"Ready for your DRE today?" I inquired.

"Not yet," he replied as he reached into the bag and withdrew a shot glass, a strip of leather and a bottle of Jack Daniels. I looked on with interest as he cracked the seal on the bottle and poured a generous portion into the shot glass. Then, as in a scene from an old western movie, he downed the shot, picked up the leather strip and clamped it between his teeth. He turned his back to me, pulled down his pants and through gritted teeth announced, "I'M READY NOW!"

It was a full two minutes before my own laughter subsided enough to allow me to get on with the exam. Kudos to Ross, who transformed a potentially awkward ordeal into a hilarious career spanning memory.

In family medicine, there are times when cracking a joke feels about as appropriate as using a vice grip to pick up a robin's egg. But occasionally, humor turns out to be the perfect tool despite the fragility of the situation.

After years of family practice, you don't only end up with a list of patients; you've got a collection of extended family members. You share experiences and take interest in each other's lives. You celebrate the birth of a child, a promotion, or simply talk about a recent vacation.

There are also difficult times such as a divorce or a death in the family. Our job as Family Doctors is to help patients cope with those traumas. The greatest challenge exists when one of our patients becomes terminally ill.

It is with the fondest of memories that I recall 'Norm' one of my favorite patients. He was about 15 years my senior and routinely pointed out his wrinkles and receding hairline. He would then grin and announce, "Take a close look, this is you in the future!"

No topic went unexplored during his visits which always stretched past their allotted time. I'd look at my watch, sigh, and then dive back into conversation, because hanging out with him was worth a little schedule chaos.

When Norm was diagnosed with end stage cancer, I was the one who cared for him and, ultimately, admitted him to hospice.

Ever the natural comedian, Norm possessed a sense of humor that bordered on insane and was somehow contagious. Whether intentional or not, he turned every visit I paid him at hospice into a contest to see how long he could make me stay. I rarely escaped in under thirty minutes.

That kind of time affords you the luxury of letting your guard down and living in the moment. Our discussions were wide ranging and occasionally strayed into the topic of mortality.

We laughed together about the fact that neither of us knew what happens after death. He one-upped me by boasting that he would get that answer first. I responded that if he were a true friend, he would let me in on his enlightenment.

He was uncharacteristically quiet for a moment and then, with an evil smile retorted, "I will be your personal poltergeist. Then you will know for certain that there is something after death!"

"Thanks," I responded, "but how about just some gentle haunting, maybe just move some furniture around?"

In those moments, we balanced on that razor's edge between

laughter and tears, finding comfort in our shared, distorted sense of humor.

And you know what? I think it helped. He was able to face the end with a grin instead of a grimace, and I managed his loss with a little less pain. As I reminisce about Norm, it is the laughter that resounds louder than the tears.

The last story I would like to share involves my own experience as a patient.

The last thing I remember before being put under, was the burning sensation in my arm from the passage of the anesthetic.

I woke up in the recovery room feeling warm and comfortable. My attentive nurse told me I was wakening following brachytherapy, a procedure for treatment of prostate cancer.

With the kind of poor decision making common to those who have had one too many, I attempted to be witty with the nurses while my brain slowly rebooted. My first comments about being a few bricks short of a load, were just lame, but I was just warming up and soon began telling cement-time jokes.

The nurses were required by their employment to remain close, so it was the perfect captive audience. I knew that if I was accused of inappropriateness, I could blame it on the anesthetic.

While the average length of stay in recovery is two-three hours, I enjoyed the experience so much, I stayed more than five hours. Why did I have the extended recovery room visit, you ask? Well, to be discharged home, you must first demonstrate that you can pass urine.

I was eager to get this under way and so had managed to drink about a liter of water and received more fluids through an IV.

Once I had demonstrated to the nurses that I was able to walk, they escorted me to a private bathroom and gave me a plastic jug to collect the urine. There would have to be proof of my success before sending me home.

For those who do not know me, this would be the time to confess that I am a fainter. Twice in my life I have fainted and have had numerous near-fainting episodes. They typically occur at particularly inconvenient times.

Let's focus back on the bathroom. I was reminded before being left alone, not to lock the door and to pull the red alarm cord if I needed any assistance.

I sat on the edge of the toilet and positioned the jug to capture my prize. Then with focused concentration, tried to relax and let things flow. To my disappointment, I could not produce a single drop. The room began to spin. Sensing the inevitable loss of consciousness, I swiftly executed an emergency maneuver - I dropped to the cool tiles below where I lay sprawled like a discarded rag doll. In hindsight, I should've summoned aid with the pull of a cord, but pride and a severe shortage of blood flow to my brain conspired against such sensible action.

Eventually the nurse knocked on the door to see how I was doing. I admitted that I was lying on the floor.

The extremely caring staff helped me back to my bed and did not give me the scolding I so richly deserved.

I spent the afternoon hydrating and telling jokes.

When I ran out of jokes, and I have a lot of them, it was time to give it another try. Once again, I positioned myself at the edge of the throne and with one hand holding the red alarm cord, visualized waterfalls and rain drops. It felt like an eternity, but in the end, I have never been so proud of a bodily function. Returning to the nursing station I held my jug of golden liquid aloft, as if it was an Olympic medal.

Basking in the nurses' effusive praise, I was allowed to arrange my ride home. That night I slept like a baby....I was up EVERY hour.

All that hydration had to go somewhere.

I know this is a joke book and this last chapter may seem a little out of place. I justify its inclusion because as a physician I want people to be healthy. If we learn to see the humor in our daily lives, including the difficult challenges, then my prescription for laughter can be filled every day.

My Parents wanted me to be a comedian.
I've been such a disappointment.

Acknowledgements

Thank you to Dr. Derek Plausinis for introducing me to the concept of the cement-time joke. I hope by giving him top billing in the acknowledgements he will forgive me for not naming the book 'Cement-Time Jokes'. I further ask his pardon for ignoring his suggestion that I include a chapter titled 'Jokes that did not make it past my censor'.

A special thank you to the operating room nursing staff and department of anesthesiology at Kelowna General Hospital who have been my audience and co-conspirators in this hilarious adventure.

My sincere thanks to all my friends and family-practice patients who have shared their humorous material.

I am indebted to Nancy Wise at Sandhill Book Marketing Ltd. who provided encouragement and mentoring throughout the preparation of this edition of the book. Regina McCreary, a skilled book designer, is responsible for giving the book its finishing touch.

I must acknowledge that I have authored only a few of the jokes in this collection. I am grateful to the many generations of joke writers who see the world differently and share their humorous insights.

My children, Robert, Aidan and Ben, endured their journey into adulthood during the building of my joke obsession. If there is any money to be made in this publishing, I will see to it that their trauma counselling be covered.

And finally, to my wife Lauri, for listening to all of the jokes, editing my stories, for tolerating my hundreds of requests for opinions and rejecting the jokes that should not be told, I cannot express the depth of my gratitude. I suspect you are the only reason I have avoided that meeting with the hospital Chief of Staff…so far.

A note from Prostate Cancer Foundation Canada

Since being formed by prostate cancer patients in 1997, Prostate Cancer Foundation Canada (formerly Prostate Cancer Foundation BC) has been providing grassroots leadership and resources for prostate cancer support, awareness, and research.

Why prostate cancer? It's the most diagnosed cancer in men, not only in Canada, but in more than 110 countries worldwide. This translates into 1 in 8 Canadian men diagnosed with prostate cancer in their lifetime. Our goal is to make sure that no one ever has to feel like they are going through this alone.

With a small staff and the support of hundreds of volunteers, whether it's through our fundraising efforts to ensure research scientists can continue their life-saving work, or creating and providing resources, free of charge, to assist men and their loved ones, we are here for you.

Some of the services we provide:

Reef Knot Kits: The more men know about their prostate cancer, the better able they will be to make informed decisions. Our free information kits are distributed to newly diagnosed patents and healthcare providers across Canada.

Support Groups: Our 5 nationwide and 60 local groups provide a safe and comfortable environment where patients and partners can ask questions and hear presentations from leading experts. Our nationwide groups include: Coast to Coast, Active Surveillance, Advanced, Partners.

One on One Peer Support: For those who aren't prepared for a group setting, we connect patients and partners with other patients and caregivers who have been on this journey too, navigating treatments and side effects, for a confidential chat.

If I Were Tom: A unique interactive website, IfIweretom.ca is an excellent interactive tool for men wanting to plan their next steps after diagnosis.

Butts in Motion: Our fitness website buttsinmotion.com includes free yoga, free exercise classes, walking clubs, and three dragon boat teams in Vancouver, Toronto, and Moncton.

Research grants: We provide grants to research scientists in BC and Ontario.

Prostate Cancer Foundation Canada offers support for everyone, for every stage of your journey, no matter where you live.

www.prostatecanada.ca

Manufactured by Amazon.ca
Acheson, AB